12 Disciplines of
LEADERSHIP
EXCELLENCE

How Leaders
Achieve
Sustainable
High
Performance

BRIAN TRACY
DR. PETER CHEE

New York   Chicago   San Francisco   Lisbon   London   Madrid   Mexico City
Milan   New Delhi   San Juan   Seoul   Singapore   Sydney   Toronto

1 2 3 4 5 6 7 8 9 10   QFR/QFR   1 9 8 7 6 5 4 3 2

ISBN   978-0-07-180946-7
MHID   0-07-180946-5

e-ISBN   978-0-07-180947-4
e-MHID   0-07-180947-3

Library of Congress Cataloging-in-Publication Data
Tracy, Brian.
    12 disciplines of leadership excellence : how leaders achieve sustainable high performance / by Brian Tracy and Peter Chee.
        pages cm
    ISBN-13: 978-0-07-180946-7 (alk. paper)
    ISBN-10: 0-07-180946-5 (alk. paper)
    1. Leadership. I. Chee, Peter. II. Title. III. Title: Twelve disciplines of leadership excellence.
    HD57.7.T715 2013
        658.4'092—dc23   2013002501

Leadership

McGraw-Hill books are available at special quantity discounts to use as premiums and sales promotions or for use in corporate training programs. To contact a representative, please e-mail us at bulksales@mcgraw-hill.com.

This book is printed on acid-free paper.

This book is fondly dedicated to Joe Traina, one of the finest and most excellent leaders I have ever known. His ability to achieve outstanding business results in the face of every adversity is a continuous inspiration to everyone who knows him.
—B.T.

To Eunice and Adelina for bringing out the best leader in me and for your everlasting love.
—P.C.

CONTENTS

INTRODUCTION

*"Leaders establish the vision for the future and set
the strategy for getting there."*
—John P. Cotter

Your ability as a leader to master the 12 Disciplines of Leadership Excellence explained in this book can do more to help you rise to the top of your field than perhaps any other single factor.

Self-discipline is the essential quality for success in any endeavor. After 22 years of interviews and research into the 500 richest and most successful men in America, Napoleon Hill concluded that self-discipline was the "Master Key to Riches." With self-discipline, everything is possible. But without self-discipline, virtually nothing is possible.

The leadership disciplines described in this book are learned qualities that require tremendous determination and persistence to develop and maintain. The good news is that each of these disciplines is learnable with repetition and practice. As Goethe wrote, "Everything is hard before it is easy."

The development of an essential discipline is hard work and more hard work initially, involving two steps forward and one step back. But once you have developed a particular discipline, it becomes automatic and easier to practice throughout your career.

Self-discipline is the essential quality of character—the ability to withstand the temptation to compromise in any area. It is the true test of the person you have become to this date. Is it worth it? Jim Rohn wrote, "Discipline weighs ounces; regret weighs tons." Al Thomsick, the teacher and trainer, once wrote that "Success is tons of discipline."

Develop a Long Time Perspective

Dr. Edward Banfield of Harvard conducted more than 50 years of research into the reasons for upward socioeconomic mobility in the United States and in other countries. He concluded that the most important single factor to predict success was what he called "long-term perspective." He defined long-term perspective as the ability to think forward into the future, and then to come back to the present day, the present moment, and use that future vision or goal as a criterion against which to measure present actions or decisions.

Leaders have a long time perspective. They project forward 1, 2, 3, 5, and even 10 or 20 years into the future when deciding on a current course of action. They take the time to carefully consider the potential consequences of an act or a behavior before they engage in it. They practice "back-from-the-future" thinking.

Denis Waitley, the business speaker, wrote about top people and time perspective by saying that, "They plant trees under which they will never sit." The difference between a politician and a statesman is that the politician plans for the next election; the statesman (or woman) plans for the next generation.

One of the top business books of the 1990s, *Competing for the Future,* by Gary Hamel and C. K. Prahalad, said that the major job of the executive or leader was to determine the "future intent" or long-term goals for the business. They said that clarity about future intent sharpens and improves current decision making.

Peter Drucker said that the primary job of the executive was to "think about the future, because no one is tasked with this responsibility."

Milton Friedman wrote, "The quality of your thinking is determined by the accuracy of your ability to predict the long-term consequences of your current actions."

Henry Hazlitt, the economist, said that the ability to determine the secondary consequences of your actions is essential to good decision making.

Self-Discipline Is a Learnable Quality

Many people feel that they lack self-discipline in certain areas and they often assume that, "That's just the way I am." Are some leaders born with natural qualities and abilities that make self-discipline easy for them? Peter Drucker addressed this question when he said, "There may be such a thing as natural-born leaders, but there are so few of them that they make very little difference in the great scheme of things." He went on to say that "Leaders are made by development, primarily self-development."

The fact is that you can develop any discipline or habit that you consider to be desirable and necessary. For some people it will be easier, and for others it will take more time and effort. But each person has the inborn ability to shape his or her character and personality in a positive way by being clear about his or her future intent and determined enough to press forward through the inevitable difficulties, resistance, and setbacks.

Develop the Disciplines You Desire

The process of developing a leadership discipline is simple, though not easy. Nothing worthwhile is easy.

First, decide upon the one discipline that can be most helpful to you in your career at the moment. Don't try to change several things about yourself at one time or to develop several disciplines for yourself simultaneously, no matter how attractive and desirable they may be.

Your basic need is to focus and concentrate on the development of a *single* discipline until it is locked in and becomes a part of your personality. Then you can move on to the development of the next discipline on your list.

The good news is that every act of discipline strengthens and reinforces all your other disciplines. At the same time, every weakness in discipline weakens your other disciplines. You must be vigilant. *Everything counts!*

Your first discipline could be something as simple as *punctuality*, or pausing before immediately replying in a conversation or a meeting. It can be as simple as flossing your teeth each day, or arising early and exercising each morning before you begin your day. The cumulative effect of developing small disciplines enables you to develop larger, more important disciplines later.

Program the New Discipline Into Your Mind

Once you have chosen a discipline to develop, begin to think about how you would behave if you had this discipline or habit already. See yourself acting or reacting in a situation where you want to practice this discipline.

Then, create a positive affirmation for yourself to continually reinforce the new discipline. You will actually *become* what you say to yourself about yourself over and over again.

For example, you could repeat the affirmation "I am always early for every meeting and appointment." Each time you think of a meeting or an appointment, or find yourself delaying, repeat those words over and over again; "I am always early for every meeting and appointment." You could also say, "I stop, pause, and think before I reply." In each meeting or discussion, say these words to yourself to remind yourself to think before you say anything.

Launch Your New Discipline Strongly

Once you have decided on the discipline you are going to develop, the key is for you to launch strongly on your new discipline. Resolve to never allow an exception until it becomes permanent. If you "fall off the wagon," immediately restate your affirmation or command to yourself and begin again.

Tell *others* that you are working to develop a particular new discipline. Telling others and knowing they are watching you will motivate you to practice the discipline. Give them permission to remind you if you forget from time to time, as you probably will.

Promise *yourself* that you will persist in the development of this new discipline until it becomes a habit. The key to success has always been to "Form good habits and make them your masters."

Resolve to persist in the development of your new discipline for 21 days, without exceptions. Twenty-one days is the average time that it takes for you to develop a new habit pattern of medium complexity. But be aware that for some people, the development of a leadership discipline may take weeks or months, or even years.

The good news is that what was difficult at first will become natural and easy over time.

Fight the Temptation of the Path of Least Resistance

The great enemy of self-discipline is the natural human tendency toward taking the path of least resistance, toward *expediency*. Most people spend every moment seeking the fastest and easiest way to get the things they want *right now*, with little or no concern for the secondary consequences of their actions.

The only brake on this human drive toward immediate gratification is self-discipline and the qualities of character, which we will talk about later in this book.

Remember the importance of a long time perspective. Consider the consequences of your words or behaviors before you act. Don't be impatient with yourself or expect to change the habits of a lifetime quickly and easily.

Instead, settle in for the long term. In one year, which will pass quite quickly, by developing one new discipline per month, you can develop each of these leadership disciplines and remake yourself into a completely different person.

Persistence and Self-Discipline

The best part of this process of developing leadership disciplines is the direct relationship between self-discipline and *persistence*. The more you persist, in any endeavor, the greater self-discipline you will develop. It has been well said that "Persistence is self-discipline in action."

Another direct relationship can be seen between self-discipline and the qualities of self-esteem, self-confidence, and personal pride. The more consistently you practice your chosen disciplines, the more you will like and respect yourself. You will feel more confident and optimistic. You will become more effective in every area of your life.

When you develop the disciplines of leadership excellence, you will become a more powerful and resourceful leader, get more done, and succeed at higher levels in everything you attempt.

Let's begin.

CHAPTER 1

THE DISCIPLINE OF LEADERSHIP EXCELLENCE

"Leadership consists not in degrees of technique but in traits of character; it requires moral rather than athletic or intellectual effort, and it imposes on both leader and follower alike the burdens of self-restraint."

—Lewis Lapham

The great Supreme Court Justice, Oliver Wendell Holmes, once said that there are three types of people: the people who *make* things happen, the people who *watch* what's happening, and the people who haven't the slightest *idea* of what's happening. In this chapter, we will talk about leadership in action and about the people who make things happen.

Today, as never before, our society is experiencing a pressing need for leadership. This need for leadership can be felt in our homes, in our business organizations, in our private and public associations, and in our government. We need leadership more than ever before. And we especially need leadership to take us into the future. We need people who have vision, who have courage, people with the ability to chart new seas and break new ground.

We need two types of leaders. The first type of leader that we need is the *transformational leader*. This leader is a pathfinder, a visionary.

This leader motivates, uplifts, inspires, and empowers people to perform at levels far beyond anything they've ever done before.

The second type of leader we need is perhaps the most important or foundational; what is called the *transactional leader*. The transactional leader is the person who gets things done with and through others.

The World Has Changed

We need leadership badly in our organizations because of the type of people in these organizations. People today are far more difficult and demanding, far more impatient and selfish than they have ever been before.

It's no longer enough just to give a person a job and to tell them what to do. People want to participate. They want to discuss their jobs. They want regular feedback on their performance. They want to know, "What's in it for me?" Today, more and more, when people go out to look for a job, especially *talented* people, and members of Generation Y, instead of them approaching their job search politely and obsequiously, their attitude is, "Why should I work for you?"

One of the major reasons that people go to work for any organization is because of the leadership. So what exactly is leadership? Two excellent definitions of leadership apply especially to business organizations. The first one is:

Leadership is the ability to elicit extraordinary performance from ordinary people.

Another definition is:

Leadership is the ability to get followers.

Today we find that the only lasting kind of leadership is not leadership that comes from position, or from money or authority. It is what we call *ascribed* leadership, which occurs when people decide for themselves that they are going to follow the direction, the guidance, and the vision of someone else. In other words, it is a *voluntary* form of following that marks our best leaders today.

Leaders Are Made, Not Born

Leaders are made, not born. Nobody comes into the world as a natural leader. A person becomes a leader by, first of all, deciding to become a leader, and second of all, by learning the skills necessary to "elicit extraordinary performance from ordinary people."

Along a continuum of personalities at the very bottom are people who haven't the slightest idea what is going on, and who couldn't care less. Then at the very top are those 1 or 2 percent of people in our society who really are the spark plugs in the engines of change. Every one of us is on that scale somewhere, moving up or down depending upon the things that we are doing and saying on a daily basis.

You are what you *think* you are. Your self-concept determines your performance. You can become a much more effective leader by changing your self-concept, by changing the way you think about yourself as a leader.

Select Leaders to Emulate

The starting point of becoming a better leader is to begin thinking about the leaders you know, who you admire, and then to think about how you could emulate their behaviors. Think about how you could be more like them. In no time at all, you will actually begin to imitate their qualities and behaviors, and become a better leader yourself.

All great leaders were at one time good followers. All great leaders at one time worked closely with other successful leaders and learned from them and emulated their behaviors.

The study of great leaders of the past and present is one of the fastest and surest ways to develop leadership qualities. The more you study what constitutes effective leadership, the more likely you will be to internalize the same values and behaviors. These values and behaviors will then be externalized in your actions and in your results.

Alexander the Great

The story of Alexander the Great is instructive for anyone who aspires to a high leadership position. By the age of 15, Alexander was convinced that it was his destiny to conquer the entire known world. He had a vision of uniting all mankind in a common brotherhood. With Aristotle as his teacher, he studied and prepared himself for many years. He learned the military arts from his father and his father's best generals. He saw himself as a great king and had an unshakable belief in his ability to achieve any goal he ever set for himself.

Alexander was brilliant at both administration and execution. He showed great judgment in delegating, and appointed the right officers in the right positions at the right time. He was able to plan, organize, think through, and execute brilliantly.

At the Battle of Arbela, he led his 50,000 men in a full frontal assault on the 1 million–strong Persian army and routed them. He never entertained the possibility of defeat. He trusted completely in himself, in his men, and in their ability to overcome any difficulty, no matter how great the odds against them.

Alexander, like all great leaders, had the ability to organize his men and inspire them to exceed anything they had ever done before. He had the ability to concentrate on his strengths and to focus on the critical areas that were essential for victory. His life and history are an example of the blending together of all the great leadership qualities that have been identified in almost every study on the subject.

A Sense of Mission

Leaders have a vision and a sense of mission that lifts up and inspires men and women to achieve that mission. In almost every person is that desire to commit to something bigger than one's self. Leaders have the ability to tap into that root source of motivation, drive, and enthusiasm that enables people to commit themselves to achieving that vision.

As a leader, you must have a goal that excites and inspires others to perform at levels higher than ever before. And the only goals that excite and inspire are goals that are *qualitative*. Nobody gets permanently excited or inspired about raising the share price or making more money or getting a raise. But we do get inspired and excited about bringing a product or service to people who need it, about being the best, and winning great success in a competitive field. Just look at the thousands of people who get caught up in an election, working long hours for little or no pay!

We need to feel that we are good at what we do, or moving in that direction. Nobody feels great or as good as they could be, nor are they capable of extraordinary performance, unless they are aligned with the best people in their field and are doing the best job they are capable of.

A big goal or inspiring mission gives a clear sense of direction not only to the organization but to every person in the organization. A desirable goal unifies everyone in a common cause. As an example, IBM is one of the greatest industrial leaders in business history. One of their goals is to give the best customer service of any company in their industry in the entire world. Everyone in the company is dedicated to this goal in every area of activity.

Apple is dedicated to producing products that people *love*. Zappos is committed to making their customers *happier* than any of their competitors. These goals are qualitative and emotional. They excite and inspire people throughout the company. People think about them and talk about them all the time. The people in top companies believe they're the best and that nobody does a better job than they do. Everyone in the company knows that their job, one way or another, is related to taking care of customers. This mission unifies everyone in a common cause.

If you are going to be a business leader, or a leader of a department or any organization, you have to sit down and think through what is going to be the mission or the overarching purpose or goal in your area of responsibility. Your determination in a mission to *be the best* at something that helps your customers and clients is the starting point of your rise to the top levels of leadership.

Take Continuous Action

When you study the life of Napoleon or Florence Nightingale or Mother Teresa or Alexander the Great, you find that they were incredibly active men and women. They were not contemplative persons who waited for things to happen. They were people who got an idea, a concept, a mission and then launched strongly and forcefully into it.

Leaders are both entrepreneurial and innovative. The word *entrepreneurial* comes from the French word meaning to *undertake* or *to do*. Entrepreneurs continually try new things. They fail fast, learn quickly, and keep moving forward. They don't analyze things to death.

They are also forward thinking. Most leaders focus their thoughts on the future—what it will be and how to create it. Most nonleaders focus on the present and the past, and who is to blame for what went wrong.

The motto of the business leader of today: "Do it, fix it, try it." Top leaders and companies tend to try more things, make more mistakes, and learn more lessons than others. They don't hesitate by spending months and years on analysis; they get out and do something.

The Quality of Courage

Courage is one of the most important qualities of leadership. Courage enables the leader to launch into new endeavors with no guarantee of success. It inspires people to rally around the banner of the leader. Courage is a habit that is learned by acting courageously whenever the quality of courage is required.

Develop Your Courage

Here are some keys to developing the quality of courage: The first is *boldness*. Whenever you feel like hesitating or backing away from a challenge, you instead force yourself to go forward. To further develop courage, practice boldness, even when you don't feel like it.

One of my favorite quotations is, "Act boldly and unseen forces will come to your aid." I have worked with many men and women who had limited talents, abilities, and resources, but who achieved great success in business because they overcame their fears and launched themselves forward boldly whenever they got an opportunity.

Somehow, when you continually launch yourself toward your goals, all kinds of things seem to work for you. Forces and people and circumstances conspire together to help you accomplish your goals in ways that you cannot now imagine or anticipate.

The demonstration of courage in a leader can be seen in the willingness to initiate action. Leaders don't wait for someone else to do something. Like a military general, leaders do not allow the enemy to determine when an attack should take place. Leaders continually take the offensive, continually move forward, continually attack. They "ride toward the sounds of the guns."

Frederick the Great

Frederick the Great of Prussia united all the smaller kingdoms of Germany for the first time. He was one of only a few people to be known as "the Great" in his lifetime. His strategy was simple: Whenever he met the enemy, no matter how great their numbers, he attacked. If you were an enemy force facing Frederick of Prussia when he discovered you, he would attack. If he had 10,000 men and you had 70,000, he would attack you. His motto was, "L'audace, l'audace, toujours l'audace,"—Audacity, audacity, always audacity.

Of course, he lost many battles, but he won the critical ones. He created the powerful kingdom of Prussia and was one of the foremost rulers of his day. Other leaders knew that if they challenged him, he would always attack with all his forces to defeat them. As a result, no rival king or general would challenge him in his later years.

Stay the Course

One mark of courage is the ability to stay the course, often called *courageous patience*. It is what Margaret Thatcher as prime minister of Britain was famous for. She was brave and tenacious, taking on the entire political establishment of her time to bring Britain back to pride and prosperity.

No matter how tough it gets, no matter how much tension or stress you face, *stay the course* and hang in there. If you refuse to give up, the sun will eventually break through the clouds and good things will happen for you.

Remember that the future belongs to the *risk takers*. Life holds no greatness for those who avoid taking risks. Of course, it doesn't mean that you take foolish risks or risks where you cannot afford the costs of a loss. It simply means that you must continually take calculated risks in the direction of your most important goals.

Smart risk takers do everything possible to *minimize* risks. They get all the information they can, which enables them to make informed decisions. They consider the worst possible thing that may occur before they commit and take action, but then they dare to go forward. Perhaps no other quality distinguishes leaders from nonleaders more than their willingness and their daring to push forward, and to keep pushing.

The Leader as Strategist

Leaders are good strategists and planners. Successful men and women in business seem to be especially good at considering all the factors involved in a course of action. They have learned how to do *strategic thinking*.

Strategic thinking means taking the long view. It means engaging in "big picture thinking." It requires carefully considering what you are doing and the different things that could potentially occur. Leaders continually ask: "If we do *this*, what is likely to happen? How will my competition respond? What will the market do?"

Part of strategic thinking requires the practice of *teleological* thinking. This type of thinking involves projecting forward and assessing the different possible outcomes and results of your actions *before* acting. It was said that Napoleon won most of his battles in his tent. He would look at the plan of battle and his maps and consider the various things that could go wrong. He would then think through what he would do in response to each of those events, should they occur. In the heat of the battle, when the enemy acted unexpectedly or the battle started to go against him, he remained calm and in command. He had already thought through each contingency and was able to respond quickly with new orders to redeploy men, artillery, and cavalry to counter the threat or take advantage of the opportunity.

People who think strategically always have an advantage over those who fail to think through the possible consequences of their actions in advance.

Concentrate Your Forces

A key element of strategic thinking is to concentrate your forces. Identify clearly the strengths of yourself, your people, and your organization and focus them where they can make a major difference, where you can win market in the market. You focus your strengths on the greatest opportunities in the marketplace where you can gain significant competitive advantage.

It is rather pointless to go head to head with strong and entrenched competition. But numerous opportunities can be found in the marketplace for a company to maximize its unique qualities, differentiate its products and services, and go after a specific market segment where its competitors are weak and where you can develop superiority, where you can win battles.

You must also give thought to what we call the WPO—the worst possible outcome. What's the WPO that could occur in terms of problems or setbacks? What's the WPO that could occur in terms of changes in market demand, interest rates, staff makeup, and the actions of your competitors? Think these things through so that if conditions change dramatically and unexpectedly, you will be prepared with a backup plan.

Strategic thinkers and leaders have the ability to react quickly because they have thought through what is likely to happen and prepared for it. They're not shaken or knocked off balance by negative events. They have the ability to see clearly, to take in the situation and make decisions to redeploy assets and people, to back off in some areas and move forward in others. In many cases your ability to react quickly to an adverse circumstance is the key to success in leadership.

Look for Opportunities

Much leadership is *situational*. Many leaders rise to the top because a situation created a great opportunity, and they recognized it as such. Many men and women have worked for many years in average positions, and then, because they acted quickly and effectively in a period of turbulence or adversity, have suddenly been promoted into a leadership position.

Many people who have been competent leaders in one situation have turned out to be poor leaders in another situation. Some people are good leaders under stable conditions, and others are excellent under turbulent conditions.

Today in America, one type of executive is called the "turnaround artist." This person is an expert in a situation when a company is in danger of collapsing due to serious problems, usually with sales and profitability. The company owners or directors, usually as a last resort, bring in a turnaround specialist to reorganize and get the company back to profitability in a matter of a few months, which all the efforts of its existing leadership could not do it.

Leadership is highly situational, and the qualities that are necessary for success differ. But in every case, it is *adversity* that uncovers great leaders. It is adversity that reveals whether a leader is truly competent. Whenever you face an adverse situation, and everything starts to fall apart around you, remember that it can be an opportunity to demonstrate you have "the right stuff" necessary to be a leader.

The Ability to Inspire and Motivate

The average person in the workplace operates at less than 50 percent of capacity. Leaders are those who have developed the ability to draw that 30, 40, or 50 percent of additional capacity out of the average person and get them to contribute far beyond their previous levels of performance.

Leaders have several different ways in which they inspire and motivate. One way is to arouse *enthusiasm*, which frequently comes by being enthusiastic themselves. A one-to-one relationship is often evident between how excited and enthusiastic you are about what you're doing and how excited and enthusiastic you can make other people. If you are tremendously enthusiastic personally, people around you are much more likely to feel the same way.

Another way to inspire and motivate is through *commitment*. Leaders are 100 percent committed to the success of the business. They are *all in*. They have a sense of total commitment to their work. That personal level of commitment will determine the level of commitment of those around them.

The level of commitment will also determine the attention received from superiors. Highly committed people are always considered more valuable to an organization and preferred when it comes to additional responsibilities and promotion over those who are not.

People who run their own businesses will find that their level of enthusiasm and commitment to their own company, to their products, and to serving their customers is a key determinant of whether they become leaders in their field.

Leaders *empower* others through their ability to make others feel more powerful with the generous use of *encouragement*. When you remember the stories of George Washington at Valley Forge encouraging his soldiers, Napoleon marching with his soldiers into battle, and Alexander sleeping with his troops in the field, sitting around campfires and telling his troops how much he believed in them, you recognize encouragement as a powerful tool in inspiring and motivating others.

Leaders inspire trust and confidence. And this trust and confidence leads to the wonderful discovery that if you really believe in your own leadership abilities and the leadership of the people you report to, you will accomplish results far beyond anything you can imagine today.

Leaders inspire *loyalty* by being loyal to their companies and to their people. Loyalty is the cement that binds an organization together. It is vital to the success of any organization. Leaders inspire others to become loyal and committed to the success of the business, by setting a good example.

Commitment to Winning

Why do people follow leaders? What enables average men and women to elicit extraordinary performance from average people? Why do people confer the title of *leader* on an individual? The simple explanation is that people become leaders because they are viewed as the individuals most likely to lead the organization to "victory" in a competitive market.

Leaders are determined to win, to succeed in achieving the company's goals of increased sales, growth, and profitability. The main task of leadership is *victory*. When companies are losing, when they are behind in whatever category is considered critical at the moment, they replace the executive with someone else whom they believe can lead them to victory. The ability to instill in others the belief that they can win and then to lead them to that place—victory—is the key to unlocking your power as a leader.

Leaders never use the word *failure*. They think in terms of *valuable lessons*, of learning experiences, and in terms of temporary setbacks, but they never think in terms of failure. For leaders, "failure is not an option."

The Formula for Success

Thomas J. Watson of IBM was once asked by a journalist, "How can I get ahead more rapidly in my career?" Watson replied, "To be more successful *faster*, you must *double* your rate of failure. Success lies on the far side of failure." In other words, the more often you fail, and learn from your mistakes, the more rapidly you will succeed.

Some leaders even make comments such as "We have to fail faster around here if we want to succeed in our market." In other words, we have to get to our lessons quicker. Instead of one or two failures a year, experiencing 10 or 20 will make it more likely you will learn what you need to know to dominate your market.

Leaders are committed to excellence and to quality because excellence and quality lead to winning. When people go into the marketplace with a product or service, the one thing they want to know is that they are representing the best. The levels of quality and service extended to customers are important to those offering up a product or service.

Leaders believe that their organizations are capable of being the best in a given field. Their aim is to make their organization superior to their competitors. They don't want to be just as good as someone else or not quite as bad as someone else. They want to be the best.

The final part of winning is to think continually in terms of *success*, and to think about how to achieve success all the time. One of the great truths in this life is that you *become what you think about most of the time*. If you think about success all the time, then it is almost inevitable that you will be successful. If individuals within an organization continually think of increasing sales, boosting profitability, and lowering costs, prosperity and success in the marketplace will be inevitable.

Leadership is future oriented rather than problem oriented. Leaders are always thinking in terms of what to do tomorrow. What are our goals? Where do we go from here? What are our obstacles? How do we remove them? How do we fix or improve our situation? How do we change it? Instead of focusing on who is to blame, or what happened, or what's the problem, leaders need to be thinking about what to do now, in one hour, and tomorrow.

The Leader as Communicator

The ability to communicate well is a core quality of leadership. Effective leaders articulate their views, their strategies, and their visions for the business with clarity. Wherever you find an organization that could be considered unhappy or drifting, you will find a fuzzy understanding of the reason for doing the job in the first place. In a successful organization everybody knows what it is they're trying to accomplish, where they're going, and what their future is likely to be if they are successful in their efforts.

If you want to be a great leader, learn how to express your views, ideas, and goals clearly to other people. Make sure that everybody who will be helping to achieve those goals knows what they are expected to contribute.

The number one complaint of employees in the workplace today is *not knowing what's expected*. It's amazing how many people are uncertain about exactly how to make their best contribution. People who are unsure about what they should be doing soon become insecure, engage in politics, and become demotivated. They become incapable of making their maximum contribution to the organization.

Tell Them the Reasons

Leaders also communicate reasons. As much as anything else, leaders make sure people know why they are doing what they are doing. Everyone in today's workforce needs to know the rationale for doing a particular job. It's not enough for people to be told that *this* is what you're going to do. They want to know the reasons. They want to know how it affects them and how it affects their customers and other people.

The more you tell people why they are doing what they are doing, the more motivated, committed, loyal, dedicated, and involved they become with their work. The less they know about the reasons behind their work, the more indifferent they become.

You can actually *release* more of the potential in others just by telling them why they are doing their job and the difference that it makes. It doesn't even have to be a good reason, as long as it is a reason.

Leaders are excellent *low-pressure* salespeople. Leaders are always selling. They sell people on the organization, on the vision, on the goals, and on the reasons. They sell people on working longer, harder, making more valuable contributions, coming on board, and taking greater responsibility. All great leaders can sell.

In addition to being able to sell, leaders are continually negotiating. They have the ability to compromise when necessary by finding win-win solutions. A key job of leadership is to take people with different points of view, with different needs and different attitudes, and harmonize those points of view so that they all work together in cooperation to achieve the goals of the organization.

Instill Meaning and Purpose

As human beings, we need meaning and purpose as much as we need food and water and air. We need a sense of significance. Good leaders are those who make us feel valuable and important. They make us feel that what we are doing has value far beyond the day-to-day work.

They make the customer of the organization the central focus. Take the example of Nordstrom: it thinks continuously about its customers, and how it can treat them so well that they come back over and over. IBM Corporation thinks and talks about its customers all the time. More and more companies today are becoming *obsessed* with their customers, both present and future. Once everybody agrees on who the customer is, and agrees that the purpose of the company is to satisfy that customer the best way possible, it becomes much easier to get everybody pulling together.

You can tell how well led an organization is with a simple test: When you are in that organization, look at and listen to how people refer to the customer. In a good organization the customers are always talked about with respect. Employees always refer to customers with pride and speak of them as really important. When a customer calls, it is an important occasion. And when a customer has a problem and someone resolves it, it is a cause for celebration. When a customer calls and is happy or satisfied with a product or service, everybody enjoys a tremendous feeling of pride and accomplishment.

Leaders Are Always Visible

If you look at the great generals and at excellent managers, you will find these leaders are always in the field. Seldom do you find them behind their desks. The further up he or she climbs the managerial ladder, the more time the individual leader spends in the field actually talking with people.

The leader should spend at least 25 percent of his or her time with customers, not behind a desk or looking at numbers and statistics, but actually out there taking care of and interacting with customers. For example, a man was buying a VCR in a computer and electronics store in Santa Clara, California a couple of years ago. An old Japanese man, whose English was poor, waited on him. As the customer was leaving the store with his VCR, a friend of his pulled him aside and said, "Do you know who that was?" *No* was the reply.

"That is Akio Morita, the head of Sony Corporation." Morita was travelling in the United States, going into stores and actually selling products so he could get direct feedback from customers.

Good military leaders are always in the field as well. The popular expression today is MBWA, which *is management by wandering around*. It means to get out of the office, walk around, talk to people, and ask what they are doing.

Building a Championship Team

When we talk about leaders being made and not born, it is important to remember that the number one quality that puts a person on the fast track to the executive suite is the ability to assemble a championship team of people who can work together to accomplish great things.

Focus on Results

Leaders are result oriented rather than activity oriented. Leaders are always thinking in terms of the results that are expected of them. They are always asking, "What results are expected of me? Where is it that

I can make the biggest contribution? What are my highest payoff tasks?"

At the same time, leaders are always conveying to others what *their* most important results are and how to pursue their highest-value tasks and activities. Leaders know that the ability to set priorities and to focus where a person can make a significant difference is the key to human effectiveness. Motivating others to set those priorities and focus in high-value areas are the key to the effectiveness of an organization and a leader.

If you are doing things that are not in your *key result areas*, and you do them extremely well, your results will still not be as valuable as if you concentrated on doing the one or two things that can make a real difference.

The Desire to Lead

Leaders have an intense desire to lead. The terms for this desire include the *royal jelly* or the *fire in the belly*. Leaders tend to be highly individualistic. They seek autonomy and are self-reliant with a high need for control. They like to make their own decisions.

However, they also recognize that in order to get to the position where they can have control and autonomy, they have to be good followers. They have to do what their superiors ask them to do, and do it well. All great generals started off in boot camp learning how to be good followers of orders.

Leaders like to take command. They love to be in control and to take charge. Many people don't want to be leaders, and not everybody needs to be a leader. But if you are meant for leadership, you will have a tremendous desire and urge to take control, to be in charge. One of your responsibilities is to prepare yourself so that you're capable of leadership when you get your chance. "He who would rule must learn to obey."

Remember, too many leaders is not the reality. Having more leaders than necessary just doesn't seem to happen; in fact, the problem is more likely to be a shortage of leaders.

Self-Esteem in Leadership

Leaders usually have high self-esteem and a positive self-image. Good leaders like and respect themselves. They value themselves and feel worthwhile. Here are some of the keys to developing high self-esteem that you need to perform at your best.

1. Good leaders are *sensitive* to others. Leaders with low self-esteem are insensitive to others. It's as simple as that. A person who is really sensitive and likes himself tends to be alert and aware of how others feel and what effect they have on other people.
2. Leaders *know* themselves. They have high levels of self-awareness. They take a good deal of time for introspection and they know what makes them tick personally. They know their own motives and why they do what they do. They are also capable of being objective with themselves, recognizing their strengths and weaknesses honestly.
3. Leaders only take on tasks that they can perform *excellently*. Because they know themselves, they will not take on a job, task, or assignment they do not have the ability to do well. They know that everything they do contributes to their overall image as a leader, so they will only take on tasks they can perform in an excellent fashion.
4. Leaders are *honest* with themselves. They are not arrogant or prideful, vain or boastful. They have the ability to look into themselves and ask, "Is this situation right for me? Is it the right thing to do at this time?"

As a result of the combination of these qualities, leaders enjoy high levels of self-esteem and self-confidence. They feel good about themselves, and feel more comfortable with others.

Lead by Example

Leaders are excellent *role models*. They continually strive to set a good example to others in their behavior and in their conduct. They are aware that others are observing them and that their behaviors and actions have an effect on the morale of their people. They know that what they say affects their staff. As a result, they do not allow themselves the luxury of discussing their doubts or fears with others.

Practice Self-Motivation

Leaders take responsibility for keeping themselves motivated. They meet this responsibility in three ways. The first is with their *vision*. Most real leaders, especially transformational leaders, those who have the ability to create the future, are dreamers. They dream of a future and of possibilities that nobody has thought of. Sometimes a true leader can see a future with crystal clarity while other people around them can't imagine it at all. Then the leaders go forward, and through planning, organizing, and bringing together the right people, they make those dreams come true.

Second, in order to motivate themselves continually, leaders set *higher* goals. We know that if you keep setting higher and higher goals, keep striving, and make sure your reach exceeds your grasp, you will stay motivated.

And finally, leaders motivate themselves by gaining the commitment of others. What leaders find is that when other people commit to a dream, they become more enthusiastic and more dedicated.

Leaders cannot depend on others to motivate them; they have to be self-motivated. And of course, being a leader is a motivating experience in itself.

Developing Leadership Qualities

Leaders are primarily self-made; they never stop growing and developing. In one of the most extensive studies of leaders, reported in their book *Leaders*, Bennis and Wiersma found that true leaders never stop learning. They don't allow themselves to fall into a comfort zone, to become complacent, or to coast on their existing knowledge and skills. They are lifelong students.

They seek out the advice of others. Even though they are usually swamped with work, they never stop taking in new information. They never stop reading business books and magazines, attending conferences, asking questions, getting into discussions, and learning more about their fields.

The keys to continuous learning are to read, study, listen to audio programs, and take additional courses. Learn from the experts; seek out the advice of others. Ask other people for the help you need. Ask for advice. Ask for counsel. Never assume that you know it all or try to learn it from the ground up. You'll never live long enough to make every mistake. Ask others and learn from them.

Leaders have peaks and valleys. They have a few areas where they are or could be excellent, and many areas where they are not particularly good at all. As Drucker said, "The purpose of organization is to maximize strengths and make weaknesses irrelevant." Good leaders build teams with people who are strong where the leader is weak, which allows them to concentrate on developing their own special strengths to even greater heights. These leaders find people who are good at things the leader doesn't like to do to free up more of the leader's time to do those things that he or she really enjoys.

Lead by Consensus

Leaders lead three ways: By command, by consultation, and by consensus.

1. A *command* decision is a decision that you make yourself after discussing it with other people.
2. The *consultative* decision happens when you ask people for their advice and input, and then you make the decision.
3. The *consensus* decision is a democratic decision. It takes place when you allow the team to make the decision and you support whatever they decide.

Leaders use all three forms of decision making. They make it clear when discussing a decision what kind of a decision it is, so that people don't think it's a consensus decision when it is a command decision, or vice versa.

When it comes to consensus decisions, a direct relationship is evident between the feeling of ownership of an idea, on the one hand, and the amount of participation the individual has had in discussing the idea, on the other. Leaders realize that the more people can discuss an idea or decision, the more likely it is that they will be committed to the implementation of that decision.

Leaders avoid giving orders whenever possible. Leaders always encourage people to think about and discuss things because they know that the more involved people become, the more deeply they will be committed to making the idea or decision successful.

Lead by Listening

Leaders are excellent listeners. As much as 50 to 60 percent of a leader's time is spent listening. The key to being an excellent listener is listening attentively, not only for the words themselves, but for what is not being said. Listen for the real message and focus all of your attention on the person who is speaking. The more intently you listen, without interrupting, the better you will understand.

At the height of the battle of Waterloo, Napoleon sent a message to Marshal Grouchy, who was in command of 30,000 crack French troops about only an hour away from the battlefield. He had to send it quickly and the messenger did not pay proper attention. The message that reached Grouchy was so unclear that he did not know what he was being asked to do. So he did nothing. He sat there with 30,000 men while Napoleon was defeated at Waterloo just a couple of hills away. The entire course of European history was changed, simply because of a lack of clarity in the message.

If you're a leader and a person wants to talk to you, close the door, turn off the telephones, and listen single-mindedly without interruption. Listening is one of the finest ways that you can learn what is really going on. A casual attitude toward listening can be disastrous for you.

Integrity: The Essential Quality of Leadership

Integrity, trust, and credibility are the foundations of leadership. Leaders stand up for what they believe in. Leaders keep their promises.

Leaders always err on the side of fairness, especially when other people are unfair. As a matter of fact, the true mark of leadership is to determine how fair you can be when other people are treating you unfairly.

The ideas and concepts of leadership discussed in this chapter are skills and abilities you can learn through decision, discipline, and practice. Here are some ways to incorporate these ideas into your work and personal life.

Action Exercises

1. List three differences in the people you manage that make your job more challenging.
2. List three leaders, living or dead, who you most admire and whose qualities you would most like to emulate.
3. List three business goals you have that are motivating and inspiring to your people.
4. Identify three ways you could demonstrate even greater courage in your day-to-day work and activities.
5. Determine three ways in which you benefit from strategic thinking and carefully considering what might happen before you take action.
6. Select three things that you could do with your staff to motivate and inspire them to higher levels of performance.
7. List three qualities you want to develop, or three behaviors that you can practice, that will make you a more effective leader.

CHAPTER 2

THE DISCIPLINE OF CLARITY

"The leader must know, must know that he knows, and must be able to make it abundantly clear to those about him that he knows."
—Clarence B. Randall

Your ability to develop absolute clarity about who you are, what you want, and the goals for your business can do more to assure your success and the success of your company than any other factor. Clarity is probably 85 percent of success, or perhaps even more. Lack of clarity is the primary reason for failure in business and personal life. People fail because they do not know who they are or what they want, or what exactly they are trying to accomplish.

The starting point of clarity as a leader is for you personally to be crystal clear about your goals—in all areas of your life. It is only when you are clear about both your personal goals and your business goals that you can focus and accomplish extraordinary things with your life.

Before you can set personal goals, you need to develop clarity about who you really are, which includes your hopes, dreams, beliefs, and personal motivations. If you are not clear about your own inner drives and motivations, you will begin to conform to and live by the wants and desires of others, which will lead inevitably to a sense of dissatisfaction and lack of fulfillment or joy in your life and work.

Determine Your Values

Your personal life is lived from the inside out. The core of your personality is made up of your innermost values and convictions, the virtues and principles that you most admire and respect both in yourself and in others. Ask yourself these questions: What are your personal values? What is it that you care about and what is important to you? What do you stand for, and what will you not stand for?

In our seminars, we ask people to identify the three to five most important values or concerns in their lives. Almost everyone begins with their family and their personal relationships. But what else is important to you? For example, do you believe in the values of integrity, courage, responsibility, spirituality, or freedom?

The next question we ask is "What would you do if you had all the money you wanted, if you were independently wealthy today?" Many people compromise their true values for a paycheck, for financial security, or to earn and keep the approval or respect of others. When you think of what you would do if you had all the money you needed, your true motivations and desires often come to the surface.

The third question we ask is, "What would you do, or how would you spend your time, if you learned today that you only had six months to live?" This question gets to the heart of ultimate "values." When you only have a short time left to live, what is really important to you in life becomes clear. As it was said, "Nobody on their deathbed ever wished that they had spent more time in the office."

Your values tell you what you will do and what you won't do in the pursuit of your other goals in life.

Select Your Goals

You need several types of goals to lead a balanced, high-performance life. Any of these goals will be more or less important to you depending on your current situation and how close you are to attaining them.

You need business and career goals, family and relationship goals, and long-term financial accumulation goals. In addition, you need short-term, middle-term, and long-term goals that will help you establish an appropriate time perspective in order to maximize your potential in each area.

Start with your business and financial goals. Practice "idealization" in each area. If you could wave a magic wand and create your ideal business and career in five years, what would it look like? How would it be different from today? What kind of money would you be earning? What kind of people would you be working with and for? What kind of a company would you be working for, and what would you be doing? What would be your ideal position and responsibilities in your career if your future was perfect in every way?

You project forward and then look back to where you are in the present, which is an exercise called "back-from-the-future" thinking. By projecting forward and looking back, you develop much greater clarity about the steps you need to take, starting today, to make your future ideal a reality.

What would have to happen for you to get from where you are to where you want to go? In particular, what is the first step that you could take today to begin achieving your business and career goals of the future?

Resolve to Take the First Step

The difference between winning and losing is almost always the willingness and ability to take the first step in the direction of your goals, dreams, and ideals. It takes tremendous courage to step out into the unknown. It takes tremendous energy for you to break out of your comfort zone and begin doing something new and different. But such a step is essential if you want to achieve your full potential as a leader.

Fortunately, once you have a clear picture of your ideal future vision for yourself, you can always see the first step. You can always see one thing that you could do immediately to begin moving in that direction. And all you have to do is take the first step.

When you take the first step in the direction of any goal, *three* wonderful things occur. First, you immediately get feedback that enables you to self-correct and change your course. Second, you immediately get insights and ideas that you can use to move even faster and further along this path. Third, you get a surge of self-confidence and self-esteem by the very act of faith in moving toward something that is important to you.

Once you take the first step, the second step will automatically appear. It seems that you can always see one step ahead. And that's all you need. If you have the discipline to keep moving toward your goal, one step at a time, you will eventually achieve it. On your journey, you will go through many twists and turns, mostly unexpected and different from what you had imagined, but you will ultimately achieve the goal if you are clear about what it will look like, and you take that first step.

Set Personal and Family Goals

The second type of goal is for your family and relationships, for your home life and the most important people in your world. As an exercise, project forward five years and imagine that your family, relationships, and lifestyle are all perfect in every way. What would your ideal life look like? Where would you be living? What kind of home or apartment would you have? How would you spend your time with the most important people in your life? What standard of living would you enjoy? What would you do day by day, week by week, and on vacations with your family?

Remember, you can't hit a target that you can't see. You cannot create a perfect future for yourself until you are crystal clear about how it would appear. Again, let your imagination flow freely. Idealize and visualize a perfect future lifestyle with the important people in your life.

Imagine that you could wave a magic wand and remove all obstacles. Imagine that you have no limitations in achieving your perfect lifestyle. When you begin to think in this way, you will begin to have all kinds of insights and ideas that will enable you to move toward your future goal, and cause your future goal to start to move toward you.

How would your future ideal be different from your current situation? And above all, what is the first step that you could take today to begin creating your perfect family life in the future? You can always see the first step.

Decide Upon Your Number

The third area of goal setting has to do with your *financial* future. Begin by deciding how long you want to live, to what age. You then determine when you want to retire, or when you will reach the point that you have enough money so that you never need to worry about money again.

A simple formula can help you determine your "number," the amount that you want to accumulate in the course of your working lifetime. The first step is to determine how much it would cost for you to live for one month at your current standard of living if you had no income at all. Most people are not clear about this number.

Multiply your monthly financial "nut" by 12 to determine how much you would need to have accumulated in order to live comfortably for one year without working. Let us say that you need $10,000 per month to live comfortably. Multiply that by 12 to get $120,000 per year. Finally, multiply your annual income requirement by 20 years to determine the exact amount of money that you will need to accumulate over the course of your working lifetime. In this case, $120,000 times 20 years works out to $2.4 million that you will have to save, invest, and accumulate before you can stop working.

Most people have no idea what their number really is. When they calculate their number using a simple technique like this one, they are shocked to find out how far away they are from the goals of retirement they have set.

The good news is that the fact that you determine your number in advance increases the likelihood of your achieving that number by five or 10 times. By using a long-term perspective with regard to your number, you can begin to evaluate every part of your financial life, especially your current expenditures, against the achievement of this number at some time in the future.

Set and Achieve Any Goal

A simple seven-step exercise can help you set and achieve any personal goal. It is powerful, practical, and gets immediate results. Here it is.

1. Decide exactly what you want. Be clear and specific. Your goal should be so clear and simple that you could explain it to a six-year-old child, and the six-year-old could tell you how close you are to achieving your goal. Simplicity is the key.

2. Write it down. Only 3 percent of adults have *written* goals, and everyone else works for them.

3. Set a deadline. If it is a big goal, set intermediary deadlines. Your subconscious mind uses a deadline as a "forcing system," working to bring you your goal 24 hours a day once you have programmed it into your subconscious mind.

4. Make a list of everything you can think of that you will have to do to achieve your goal. As you think of new tasks or items, add them to the list until your list is complete.

5. Organize your list both by sequence and priority. You organize your list by sequence by deciding the order that you will have to complete your tasks in. What do you have to do first? Which comes second? Which comes later?

    You organize your list by *priority* by determining which task is more important and which activities are less important. What are the activities that can help you the most to achieve your goal the fastest?

6. Take action on your goal immediately. Do something. Do anything. But launch. Take the first step and put the entire goal-achieving process into action.

7. Do something every day to achieve your major goal. This step is important. It is very difficult to get started on a new goal. It takes a tremendous amount of energy to break out of your comfort zone. But once you get started, it is much easier to keep going.

It takes less energy because you develop momentum that moves you faster and faster toward your goal, and moves your goal faster and faster toward you.

The 10 Goal Exercise

Here is an exercise for you for the short term. Take a sheet of paper and write out 10 goals that you would like to accomplish in the next year or so. Once you have written down these 10 goals, ask yourself this question: "If I could only achieve one goal on this list, which one goal would have the greatest positive impact on my life?"

Whatever your answer to that question, circle that goal on your goal sheet. That goal becomes your *major definite purpose* for your life right now. It becomes your focal point, your point of concentration on a day-to-day basis. Napoleon Hill once wrote, "People only begin to become great when they decide upon their major definite purpose in life."

Set Goals for Your Business

Once you are clear about your personal goals in each of the most important areas of your life, one of your chief responsibilities as a leader is to set clear, specific goals for each area of your business. As with your personal goals, you begin with your values; your *business* values. Corporate life, like personal life, is lived from the inside out. Both you and your people need clear, specific, and aspirational values around which to build a successful business. In a study some years ago, researchers identified the "Fortunate 500," the businesses in each industry that were substantially more profitable over a multi-year period than businesses that were not. What they found was that almost every business had values. But the most profitable businesses had clear, *written* values that everyone knew and lived by.

The less profitable businesses in the study, in the same industries, had values as well, but nobody really knew what they were, nor did they know how to operationalize those values in their daily activities.

Determine Your Business Values

What are your business values? What does your company stand for and believe in? These values tell you what you will do and what you won't do in the pursuit of sales and profitability. Each value should be accompanied by a statement of how you will practice that value on a daily basis. What actions will you take to demonstrate that value when you must make decisions?

A successful company that I worked with some years ago had identified the five most important values that the company stood for and then had created a statement to indicate how people in the company would practice those values. It then printed these values and value statements on plasticized cards for everyone in the company to carry and refer to when making a decision of any kind. By starting with an idea and a set of clear values, within a few years this company was doing more than $150 million in sales each year and dominating its industry in every city to which it expanded. The key people in the company were absolutely convinced that the establishment of the values prior to operation was the reason it was so successful, and why its people were so happy and productive.

Create an Action Statement

If you were asked to name an action statement you could, for example, say that your value is excellent customer service. What does your statement mean? You could then write, "We believe in excellent customer service: each person in our company is dedicated to the happiness and satisfaction of our customers and we will do anything within reason to assure their satisfaction."

This statement says it so that everyone inside and outside your business can understand, and compare their performance against it. This statement is something you can tell your customers. What are *your* values, and how do you carry them out in practice?

Whenever I have worked with corporations to discuss and agree upon their values, it never took less than half a day for everyone to discuss and agree on exactly what the company stood for, and in what order of priority. What was value number one? What was value number two? And so on.

Clarify Your Vision for Your Business

Once you are clear about your values, you then create a *vision* for the way your company will look at some time in the future. Again, you idealize and project forward five years. If your company was perfect in every way sometime in the future, what would it look like? And how would it be different from today?

Again, imagine that you have a magic wand and you could make your company perfect in every way. What would be your ideal level of sales and profitability? What kind of reputation would your company have in your marketplace for your products and services? What would customers say about your company after doing business with you? What words or phrases would they use to describe you amongst themselves and to others? What kind of leadership would you have in your company if your company was perfect in every way? What kind of people would you have, at all levels? Would your company be considered a great place to work? How would you or could you make your company into your ideal vision of it?

Agree Upon Your Mission Statement

Once you are clear about your values and your vision, you can then develop your *mission statement*. Your mission statement tells you and everyone else what you want to accomplish for your customers, for other people, how you will accomplish it, and how you will measure your success.

Your mission statement must have a goal—something that can be achieved or accomplished. In addition, it must have both a *method* and a *measure*. Your mission must be clear to everyone in your company, and to their spouses and children as well. It must also be clear to your customers so that they know what you are committed to doing for them.

Most mission statements are meaningless platitudes. They give no guidance or direction. They sound nice but are essentially useless in guiding and directing corporate behavior.

For example, a common type of mission statement would be "We are an innovative, high-energy company dedicated to making a difference in the communities we serve." What do these words actually mean to a customer? What does it tell a customer who is considering doing business with that company? Here is a better example: "Our mission is to produce high-quality electronic security systems that keep our customers safe and secure 24 hours a day."

Your mission statement should inspire and motivate your people, and should attract to you customers who want, appreciate, and are willing to pay for what you offer.

What Is Your Purpose?

Once you are clear about your values, vision, and mission, you define your *purpose*, which is the reason you are in this particular business; it is the reason that gets you up and gets you going in the morning.

Your purpose is the "why" of what you do. As the philosopher Nietzsche said, "A man with a big enough why can endure any what." Your reason *why* is your major motivator. It is what excites you about your work. It is what you love and enjoy, and what you think about most in your business. Your mission and purpose are always defined in terms of what you want for others—for your customers and for the people you serve with your products and services.

Once you are clear about your values, vision, mission, and purpose, you can then set goals for every part of your business. Perhaps the critical skill of the leader is the ability to plan, organize, and get results. It is the ability to decide on clear, specific measurable business goals and then to achieve those goals on schedule and on budget.

The most important word in business is "results." You must be clear. What results, exactly, are expected of you? How do you measure those results? All business activities can ultimately be described with numbers of some kind, usually financial numbers. As Harold Geneen once said, "Get the numbers, the real numbers. Numbers don't lie."

Decide Upon the Most Important Number

The preceding information brings us to a key concept with regard to clarity, and it is the determination of the most important number in your business. This number more accurately predicts and explains success or failure than any other number you can generate or track. Jim Collins, author of *Good to Great*, refers to this number as your "economic denominator." It is the standard or benchmark by which you measure the success of your business activities. Leaders can choose from more than 30 different benchmark numbers. If you don't choose one, or choose the wrong number, your business may never realize its full potential. It could even fail.

Most successful businesses are "numbers driven." They measure everything. They continually compare their actual numbers with their projected numbers. They watch for trends. They focus on improving the most important numbers. Most companies choose *sales* as their critical number. Others choose *profitability*. Still other companies choose return on equity, return on investment, return on sales, or sales per square foot (retail). As an example, when I was conducting seminars and selling educational products in the back of the room, the critical number for me was the exact amount of sales per person in the room. We judged and measured the effectiveness of our seminars by the amount that attendees purchased as a result of attending the seminar.

Set Standards of Performance

Each person or department requires clear goals, measures, plans, and deadlines in order to perform at their best. One of the chief responsibilities of leaders is to articulate the vision, embody the mission, emphasize the purpose, and clarify the goals for each person and department. Everyone needs to know exactly what the company is trying to accomplish and why. People need to know what they are expected to accomplish and why, and by when, and how it is going to be measured.

The discipline of clarity requires that you take the time to think, to discuss, to write things down, and to be absolutely clear about what it is you are trying to accomplish. The greater clarity that you have, and the greater clarity you can give to each person, the faster, more efficiently, and more effectively you will accomplish your business goals.

Ask the Critical Questions

Here are some important questions to help you develop greater clarity in your business:

1. What am I trying to do?
2. How am I trying to do it?
3. How well is it working?
4. What are my assumptions?
5. Could my assumptions be wrong?
6. Could there be a better way?
7. What results are expected of me?
8. What do I do now? What is my next action?

The job of the leader is to develop absolute clarity about each goal and activity necessary for the business to succeed, and then to articulate clear goals, activities, and measures to each person whose cooperation is necessary to achieve those goals.

Everyone must know exactly why they are on the payroll, what they have been hired to do, why it is important, and how it will be measured and rewarded. This information is essential for building a high-performance organization.

Strategic Thinking

Let's start by talking about perhaps the finest strategist that ever lived. I mentioned him previously. He was a man who started off as a "junior manager" in a large organization and worked his way up. His name is Alex. Alex's father was the head of the organization, and Alex admired his father, learned a lot from the man, and studied hard as he was growing up. He had great dreams and aspirations of building a big organization, far bigger than that of his father.

The Alex I'm talking about is Alexander of Macedon, who came to be known as Alexander the Great. When Alexander was 20 years old his father was assassinated. Alexander immediately became the king of Macedonia. The Macedonians were a tribe in northern Greece, a tough, hardy, militaristic race. They eventually conquered and ruled all of Greece.

Within Alexander's household, in his army and the army of his father, and within the other tribes of Greece, an enormous number of enemies competed for Alexander's position. When Alexander became king, he discovered numerous plots and conspiracies being organized to kill him and free the city states of Greece from Macedonian rule.

Take Command

Alexander immediately took command, as a new leader does. He quickly put down disloyal elements in his own army. He reorganized his kingdom, putting his own people in key positions, and defeated the armies sent against him. He became the recognized and accepted master of all of Greece at the young age of 20.

Then he set off on his mission. Alexander, like all good leaders, had a strategic plan, a mission for his organization. He wanted to bring Greek culture to all the world. He had an aggressive merger-and-acquisition plan in mind.

At the age of 15, the Delphic Oracle had told him that he could have a long life full of peace or a short life full of glory. He chose a short life full of glory. The high priestess at Delphi then told him that he could rule all the lands that he could look upon with his own eyes.

Start in Smaller Markets

So he took 20,000 men, put them on ships, and set out to fulfill his personal destiny—to rule the world. He began by invading Asia Minor, present-day Turkey. Alexander was a brilliant planner, and he had skilled generals under him. His troops were extremely well trained, well disciplined, and tough, and he won every single battle. As his armies moved through Asia Minor, they defeated each army that stood in their way.

In those days, when they fought with spears and swords, one did not fight and run away and live to fight another day. Fighting was rather final. The soldiers of the armies in the path of Alexander's advance began to hear about what had happened to the previous armies. They learned that anyone who fought against Alexander lost. And if you lost with a spear through your chest, it would be enough to ruin your whole day. So the word spread that perhaps it was a good idea not to fight with Alexander.

Alexander was also quite strategic in that he did not disrupt the kingdoms that he conquered. He left them under the rule of their own people. All he required was that they pay a tribute to Greece each year. Other than that requirement, they continued functioning much the same as before the conquest. The major difference was that now, they were under the protection of the Greek empire and the Macedonians.

Have a Merger-and-Acquisition Strategy

As his armies moved further south toward present day Lebanon, Israel, and Egypt, more and more tribes came and joined him. They gave up without a fight, deciding not to go to battle with him but instead to become part of his army and his empire. It was the original *merger-and-acquisition* strategy.

The most powerful executive, the head of the biggest empire in the world at that time, was a man named Darius of Persia. Darius had his capital in Babylon, in what is present-day Iran. He had the biggest conglomerate (empire) the world had ever seen. His empire extended from the Indus River in Pakistan all the way to the Mediterranean, throughout the Persian Gulf, and all the way up into what are today the old southern Soviet states.

Darius began hearing of an upstart renegade who had come over from Greece with a bunch of freebooters and was picking away at the fringes of his empire. Various tribes and kingdoms in the Persian empire were beginning to question to whom they should cast their lot—Alexander the Macedonian or Darius of Persia?

Deal Effectively with Competitors

Darius was a smart man. He recognized that this Alexander was a threat to his entire enterprise. He immediately sent an army of 50,000 men to attack the 22,000 men under Alexander. He ordered them to crush the upstart once and for all.

Alexander, anticipating this battle, laid out his strategy carefully. With brilliant leadership, he demolished and routed the Persian army that was sent against him. He then routed a second army sent by Darius who, upon hearing what had happened, said, "This is serious. This is the biggest single threat to my power in my lifetime. It must be dealt with decisively or there will be challenges to my strength and to Persian rule throughout the empire."

Darius then sent his messengers to all the tribes in his empire, ordering them to send him levies of their best troops to meet him at a place called Arbela. He sent demands for troops to many smaller kingdoms as well. These tribes sent thousands of their best troops to meet him at Arbela in present-day Iraq to fight Alexander.

Plan for Competitive Response

Alexander had acceded to the throne of Macedonia in 336. Three years later, in 333 B.C.E., he was 23 years old and had approximately 50,000 men in his army when the battle against Darius's forces took place.

Darius had assembled his army outside Arbela at a place called Gaugamela. It was the biggest army that the world had ever seen and numbered almost a million men. In all of history, even up until WWII, an army this large had never been assembled in one place. At one time, about 400 historical accounts of this battle existed. It was considered to be one of the most important battles in human civilization and a pivotal battle in the history of the western world.

Once Darius had assembled his troops, he had them clear and level the ground so that the field would be ideal for his troops and his chariots, which were his major battle force, the equivalent of tanks in modern warfare. He then sent a messenger to Alexander with something of a dare: "If you're so tough, why don't you come to Gaugamela and we'll see who's the toughest?"

Take Aggressive Forward Action

Alexander's army was positioned to the south and east in what is today Iraq. He immediately broke camp and crossed the Tigris River. The Persians under Darius thought it would take him seven days to get there but he arrived within 48 hours. His army consisted of 50,000 men and cavalry. Everyone in his army knew that the next day they would be fighting one of the biggest battles in history. Their very survival was at stake.

That night, the evening before the battle, Alexander called all his commanders together. He always explained to his soldiers everything they needed to know. He is quoted as saying, "It essential that the men who must fight the battle know what the plan of battle is."

His generals asked him what he thought was going to happen the next day. Alexander told them they were going to win. They said, "Well, sire, the men have all great faith and trust in you but you realize that according to our intelligence we are up against 20:1 odds. Darius has a million men against our 50,000."

Always Speak with Confidence

Alexander said, "Yes, I know. But I've thought this through carefully. Of course, it's not possible for us with 50,000 men to defeat an army of 1 million. However, I believe that the army of Darius is not really a single army. Instead, it's a series of perhaps 30 different armies made up of troops and levies from all over his empire.

"They have different languages, different cultures, different orders of battle, different religious rights, and different military structures. The only thing they have in common is a loyalty to Darius. I believe that if something were to happen to Darius tomorrow, the rest of the armies would divide and be more easily defeated.

"They all expect this battle to be over by lunchtime. They expect it to be a crushing defeat. So I want you to go tell all the men that we don't have to worry about defeating this whole army because we're not going to fight the whole army. Tomorrow we're going to do one thing: we're going to go out and kill Darius. Do you understand that? Tell them we're going to kill Darius."

And the word went out to the Macedonian army that night, passed on from man to man that the order of battle for the next day would be to follow Alexander and, "Kill Darius! Kill Darius! Kill Darius!"

Do the Unexpected

The next day the two armies lined up their troops. Darius organized his army like a massive wall—a million men to move forward to overwhelm and crush the Macedonians. But Alexander lined up his army differently, at an angle to the forces of Darius. This strategy, called the "oblique formation," had seldom been used, before or since. Darius had no idea how to counter it.

Darius lined up his armies in deep ranks. His major attack forces were battle chariots—with hooked swords that protruded from the wheels. Razor sharp and spinning, they would cut the legs and arms and chop through the opposing troops as they passed. If you sent 300 battle chariots into an opposing force, it would cause chaos of death and confusion, demoralizing the fighting will and ability of the opposing force. This strategy had worked repeatedly for Darius over many years, and Alexander knew Darius would use this strategy once again. The reason Darius had chosen this particular ground was because he could flatten it like a massive parking lot so his chariots could maneuver most effectively.

Having lined up his men, Alexander began to move his army to the right, away from the main battlefield and onto to rougher ground where he would have an advantage. As his entire army shifted sideways, Darius became confused. In response, Darius tried to move his army sideways to maintain his front with Alexander, which only increased the uncertainty among his soldiers.

Be Prepared for Determined Competition

Finally, Darius said, "The heck with this. Send in the chariots." The 300 battle chariots charged across the huge field between the armies, straight at the army of Alexander. But at the critical moment, Alexander had all of his men plant their shields with their spears dug into the ground. What the horses saw was a wall of shields, like a wooden wall, bristling with spears.

In battle, men will charge walls bristling with spears, but horses are different. Horses will not charge into spears or barricades. The horses and the chariots began to turn away from the wall of spears. As they turned, they began to trip each other up and cause confusion. The charioteers steered their horses away from the spears, and curved around the main body of the army and into its rear. Alexander's men were waiting with spears, swords, and archers to attack them from all sides. The charge of the chariots, Darius's main battle strategy, was demolished.

Meanwhile, the dust clouds kicked up by the chariots obscured his vision. All he could hear was the sounds of panic and pain coming from the chariots and the army behind the dust. In frustration, Darius demanded of his generals, gathered around him, "What on earth is going on over there? Has the attack succeeded? Have they broken through? Is it time to advance?"

Meanwhile, Alexander saw that his moment of opportunity, exactly as he had planned, had now come. He took his position in front of his troops, wearing white armor, a red flowing cloak, and a silver helmet with a white plume. He rode his huge black war horse, Bucephalus. He believed that a person who was confident would be victorious in the battle, and that confidence was demonstrated by leading an army from the front. He made such a striking figure that his army always knew where he was.

Choose the Right Moment

He turned to his "Companion cavalry," a special force of 6,000 men on horseback, and shouted, "Follow me and let us kill Darius!" He formed his ranks, with himself at the front, and charged straight for Darius, like a spear hurled into the ranks of the Persian army. Darius, who was directing the battle, had not anticipated this situation at all. He demanded to know what was going on. They told him, "Well sire, he seems to be coming right for you."

Darius ordered them to stop Alexander. They told him, "Well sir, we're trying to stop him but we didn't anticipate an attack straight into the front of our army. We are not prepared to repulse him."

This strategy was brilliant. The only part of Darius's entire Persian army that could fight against Alexander was the small part directly facing him. The rest of the million soldiers were of no use because they had nobody to fight against. Darius was unable to give commands to the rest of the army to move forward as long as he was facing a direct assault on his own encampment.

Again Darius shouted at his men to stop Alexander. They told him, "We're doing everything we possibly can to stop him but he continues to advance." Darius said, "If you don't stop him, he's going to break through!" None of the Persians had expected this kind of assault, and Alexander just kept cutting through the center, directly toward Darius.

A Disorderly Retreat

Darius finally said, "Well, if you cannot stop him, I must preserve my own life. You can stay here and fight with him." He then jumped into his chariot with his battle flags waving and drove off the field of battle. All around him were his generals. They said, "If you are leaving to save your life, so are we. We'll come with you." They leaped onto their horses and into their chariots and fled the field, as well.

In all the dust and confusion, and shouting and sounds of battle, the rest of the army had no idea what was happening. But they soon heard rumors that Darius was fleeing. These soldiers were not geniuses. They were simple, solid fighting men, but they could put two and two together. The first "two" was that, from everything they had heard about Alexander, he never lost a battle, and that anybody who fought against Alexander was defeated and killed, which would be a terrible way to end the day.

The second "two" was that Darius was fleeing the scene of battle. Alexander never loses, and Darius is fleeing. What could that possibly add up to? They concluded fairly quickly that they must have lost. If all was lost, then they had better escape because Macedonians were merciless with opponents and prisoners.

Alexander's analysis of the situation turned out to be correct. The units of the Persian army began to scatter and run, falling over each other to get away. At this point, Alexander, who had anticipated this reaction, began his advance. His army went through the fleeing Persians like a hay-making machine, chopping them down in huge numbers.

By the end of the day, the Persians had lost more than 400,000 men. The Macedonians under Alexander lost 1,247 men. It was one of the most lopsided and decisive battles in all of human history. With this victory, Alexander, at the age of 23, was the undisputed master of much of the known world.

The Military Principles of Strategy

Specific principles of military strategy have evolved to explain victory and defeat in warfare. These principles as developed over the centuries are taught in every military school worldwide. They are applicable to success and failure in business, as well. They are all demonstrated in the Battle of Arbela in 333 B.C.E.

The Principle of the Objective

The first strategic principle in every case is the *objective*. What is your objective? It requires knowing exactly what it is you want to accomplish. Alexander was clear about his objective. He wanted to be the master of the known world. He knew that the existing master of the known world was Darius. He knew that in order to be the master, he would have to defeat Darius. He never took his eyes off this goal.

The Principle of the Offensive

The second principle of military strategy is the *offensive*. All effective strategy is offensive, which requires that you go on the attack. No great battles in business or in life are ever won passively or defensively. The most effective strategy is called "the continuous offensive." Once you go on the attack, you never stop until you achieve victory.

The Principle of the Mass

The third principle of military strategy is *mass*. All great battles are won by the general concentrating his forces at a critical point at a critical time to take a critical strategic objective. In business, it is called *focus*, the ability to bring all your powers to bear on a decisive goal or objective.

The Principle of Economy

The fourth principle of military strategy is *economy*. You achieve your strategic objectives with the lowest possible cost, with the least amount of damage to your own forces. Achieving economy requires thorough planning in advance of committing your resources to a business goal.

The Principle of Maneuver

The fifth strategic principle is *maneuver*. You must always maintain the ability, no matter what the enemy does, to maneuver. Maneuverability requires that you anticipate what might happen to offset your plans. You develop fallback positions, the ability to move forward and back, to move sideways. You never get locked into a single plan with no flexibility, or advance with no "Plan B."

The Principle of Surprise

The sixth principle of military strategy is *surprise*. Virtually all battles are won because the attacking general did something completely unexpected, something that the defender had not anticipated. Alexander used this principle over and over to keep his opponents off balance. In product development and promotion, this principle is vital to keeping a step ahead of competitors and to achieving market dominance.

The Principle of Exploitation

The seventh strategic principle is *exploitation*. Once you have broken through, won the battle, achieved a dominant position, or taken a strong position in your market, you must move rapidly to exploit it. Destroy the opposing forces, and increase, establish, or entrench yourself with your new customers and new markets.

Setting Strategy

Four basic reasons explain why we set strategy in business:

1. To increase your *return on equity*. Strategy is defined in terms of financial results. In other words, the purpose of setting strategy is to earn a higher return on the amount of money that you have working in the company.
2. To *reposition* your company. You may find your company, your products and services, are under assault from competitors. You may find that you have to reposition your company with new products and new services in new markets with new technologies. Think about Apple between 1997 and today.
3. To *maximize your strengths* and your opportunities. Look at what it is you do extremely well and at your key opportunities in the marketplace, and then move rapidly to take advantage of them.
4. To form a basis for *making action decisions now*. The whole purpose of strategy is to prepare for taking action.

Strategic planning is not a passive activity. Strategic planning is the process of thinking through the action steps that you are going to take to achieve your goals and objectives. For you to be an effective strategic planner, you must always be thinking of the specific actions you are going to take to achieve your objectives.

Five Key Questions in Strategic Planning

Five key questions must be asked and answered over and over in strategic planning.

Question #1: *Where are we now?* What is the size of your business? What are your most important products and services? What is happening in the current market? What are your strengths? What are your weaknesses? What is your position in the market? What are your most valuable resources, and who are your competitors? What does the future look like? An accurate analysis of your current situation is the starting point of all strategy.

Question #2: *How did you get to where you are today?* What were the critical steps that you took? What did you do right? What did you do wrong? What lessons did you learn? What has changed since you began, recognizing that everything changes? What were the events that got you to where you are now?

Question #3: *Where do you want to be in the future?* In setting strategy, ask where you want to be in one year, two years, three, five, or even 10 years. Where do you want to be personally, and where do you want to be as a business? Clearly defining your future on the basis of where you are and how you got there is critical.

Question #4: *How are you going to get there?* Taking into consideration where you are, how you got there, and where you want to be in the future, what is your plan? This question and its answer are the essence of strategy.

Question #5: *What additional skills or resources will you require to achieve your strategic objectives?* Executive coach Marshall Goldsmith summarized this idea in his book, *What Got You Here Won't Get You There*. Whatever your goals for increased sales and profitability in the future, they will require that you develop new capabilities, competencies, and skills that you don't have today. What are they?

As Vince Lombardi said, when he became the head coach of the Green Bay Packers, "The key to success in football is to become brilliant on the basics." The key to success in strategic planning or in business in general is for you and your company to become brilliant on the basics of your business as well. You achieve this goal by continuing to ask and answer the right questions.

The key to strategy is not necessarily to have all the right answers but to know the right questions and keep asking them over and over again.

The Key Players in Setting Strategy

Several people need to be involved in setting strategy for the company. The first is the chief executive officer, the number one decision maker, the person who is responsible overall for the final results of the organization. He or she must be intimately involved in strategic planning. The final decision makers, the CEO, chairman of the board, or whoever is responsible for approving the strategy, must be involved in the process of developing the strategy.

The implementers are all the key players whose cooperation and active involvement will be required for the successful implementation of the strategy. These individuals are usually the senior executives of the organization, the people in charge of the major departments and functions. The more involved they are in setting of the strategy, the more likely it is that the strategy will be implemented effectively.

The more key people who are involved in the strategic planning process, the more likely it is that the strategy will be implemented and that you will achieve your goals.

Get Some Help

Strategic planning is something you cannot do by yourself. It is like dentistry, the law, or medical work. You have to find someone who is objective, who has a wide variety of knowledge and exposure to different industries, and who has studied and is experienced in strategic planning. You need someone who can come in and be a facilitator of the strategic planning process.

A good strategic planning exercise for an organization requires approximately two to four days to decide upon a new basic strategy. You need someone to help you do it. As they say with regard to law, "A person who acts as his own lawyer has a fool for a client." A person who acts as his own strategic planner probably has a fool for a client too.

Determine the Corporate Mission

The starting point of all strategy, a mission statement is always *qualitative*. It isn't "to earn a lot of money," or "to increase profitability." A mission statement is always something that uplifts and inspires people. It is a statement of what you want to accomplish for your customers.

Here is General Electric's mission statement: "General Electric is a unique, high-spirited, entrepreneurial enterprise known for its unmatched level of excellence, highly profitable with worldwide leadership in each of its product lines."

A mission statement is what is known as your "umbrella statement," the organizing principle under which everything in the company is done. The mission statement is complete when it says everthing that fits under this umbrella is what the company does, and everything that is outside this umbrella the company does not do.

If you want to add new products, services, or goals, you often have to change the mission statement. Establishing a mission statement is like getting the right combination to a lock; once you get the right combination, the lock opens. The strategy is how the mission is accomplished.

Determine Your Values

Before an organization can create any kind of strategic plan, it has to ask, "What do we believe in?" What are our essential values? The most successful companies are those that are crystal clear about their values.

IBM is a good example. IBM has three values: *excellent products, excellent customer service, and respect for the individual.* Everything in the company is organized around those three values.

What are your values? Do you value quality? Do you believe in excellence? Do you believe in taking care of people? Do you believe in market leadership or innovation? What are your fundamental beliefs about what is right and wrong inside and outside of your business?

Here is an important question to ask yourself with regard to values: What is your ideal of the how the customer views you? In other words, how would you like your customers to think about your company? Looking at you from the outside, working with you, being involved with your people, using your products and services, and then turning around and speaking to someone else, how would you like others to *describe* your company? What words would you want them to use? These questions are a good starting point for determining what your beliefs and values should be.

If the people in your company had to describe your company to someone else in terms of what kind of a company you have, what would you want them to say? What would be your ideal description if you could have your company described in any terms at all?

How do you get from where you are today, the way that you are currently perceived by your market, your bankers, suppliers, and by your own people, to where you want to be in the future, to how you want to be described at that time? This question is key.

The Driving Force: Key to Strategy

The term *driving force* comes courtesy of consultants Zimmerman and Tregoe, and is an important concept in strategy. The driving force, once determined, becomes the key principle around which all planning is done. A strategist can choose from several driving forces.

Product or Service

The first and most popular is the *product or service* driving force. The product or service driving force determines the scope of your markets and the range of your products. If for example, you were Domino's Pizza, you would have a product-driven driving force. Your entire focus would be aimed at selling more of your particular product. It is perhaps the most common driving force in business.

If your business was accounting or legal services, you would have a service-driven driving force. In other words, your entire focus would be on selling more of your services, in every way possible.

Market Needs

The second type of driving force is what is called *market needs*. Market needs are when you identify a particular market and you ask yourself, "What is it that my market needs?" You then develop or offer the products and services for that market.

One of my clients sells exclusively to the legal market. The company has set themselves up as a legal supply firm, an all-purpose firm that will supply every single product or service that a law office needs, from the time it signs its lease to the time it closes its doors. It supplies furniture, software, coffee supplies, paper, and stationery. Everything a law firm needs can be satisfied by this company, which has identified its market and produces whatever products those customers need.

Sears defines itself as being the American family's all-purpose or all-resource place to buy foods, housewares, insurance, hard goods, and so on. Its goal is to satisfy the market needs of the average American family.

Perhaps the best example of a market-needs driving force is Walmart. It defines its market as "those people who live from paycheck to paycheck." Walmart focuses on serving its customers with the products, services, groceries, and requirements that they want and need, at the lowest possible prices, and the most comprehensive guarantees of satisfaction.

Technology

A third driving force is *technology*. If you are in semiconductors, then everything that you do is determined by what applications your technology has in other products. Whether it is computers, telecommunications equipment, or satellites, your technology determines the products and services you develop, the markets you serve, and your plans for the future.

Apple is an excellent example of a technology-driven driving force. It only brings products to market that are based in its proprietary technological methods and patents.

Production Capability

A fourth driving force is *production capability*. For example, take a company that is set up to produce furniture. It has the equipment—the lathes, saws, drills, and assembly lines to produce furniture, and only furniture. Its production capability determines how much and what kind of furniture it can make. It can produce whatever its production capability may be. It can produce furniture, cabinetry, or prefabricated parts for homes, but its production capability is its driving force.

Method of Sales

A fifth driving force is your *method of sales*. It could be retail, wholesale, direct mail, distributors, MLM, or Internet-based. For example, the method of sales for McDonald's is its retail outlets. This method of sales determines all the different products it makes and the markets it serves.

Method of Distribution

Number six is a *method of distribution* driving force. For example, Avon distributes through individuals from house to house, and person to person. This method of distribution determines the products and services it can offer, the market it can serve, the prices it can charge, and everything else about its business.

Natural Resources

The seventh type of driving force is *natural resources,* which could be coal, oil, gas, timber, or other minerals. Natural resources would be the driving force for a company such as Champion International, Weyerhaeuser, or ExxonMobil.

Size/Growth

The eighth driving force is *size/growth.* Your driving force could be determined by the speed at which you want to grow. Toyota for many years has had a size/growth driving force. Its objective has been to gain market share above all else. As it gains more market share, its costs of production decrease and profits increase.

Many Japanese companies use size/growth as their key strategy. As their costs of production decrease because of economies of scale, their prices decrease. As their prices decrease, they are more competitive and their market share increases. Finally they reach the point where they have 25 percent, 30 percent, or 35 percent of the U.S. market.

Return/Profit

The ninth driving force is *return/profit.* American Home Products has a variety of different products that it offers to individuals, corporations, businesses, and families throughout the country and the world. It has one simple driving force: that every single product must have a 20 percent pretax return on sales. If the product does not have that kind of profitability because of its position in the market, the company doesn't carry it.

What Is Your Driving Force?

The selection of your driving force is absolutely critical to your future. It does not mean that you don't have other forces operating too; it just means that your primary driving force becomes the organizing principle upon which your strategy is based.

If it is *market needs*, then the products and services you offer are determined by the market you have decided to serve. Your production capability is determined by that market. *Size/growth* and *return/profit* are determined by how well you serve your chosen market, and so on. And as soon as you've determined your driving force, then you are free to go on to the next part.

Concentrate Your Powers

When we talk about concentration of power we think of the 80/20 rule. People, money and resources, and time are always limited. You cannot do everything. You must therefore concentrate on the few things that you can do well and on your best opportunities. All strategy revolves around massing your powers. You want to focus and leverage your strengths to achieve maximum advantage in the marketplace.

One of the most important of Peter Drucker's works is *Managing for Results*. In this book, he talks about the fact that 20 percent of your business will account for 80 percent of your profits, and 80 percent of your business will account for 20 percent of your profit. You always have to be looking at your business and asking yourself what is the 20 percent of your business that generates 80 percent of your profits. Remember, the cost of a business is in the number of transactions, but the profit is in the size of the transactions.

When you ask yourself what is the best part of your business to be in, you will often come to realize that you have to get out of certain parts of the business. One of the things that you ask with the 80/20 rule is "What are our key strengths?" And simultaneously you assess key weaknesses as well.

All strategy focuses on strengths and compensates for weaknesses. Ask yourself what it is that you do well, and ask yourself what you do poorly. Then, do more of what you do well and do less of what you do poorly.

Practice Zero-Based Thinking

Zero-based thinking is a strategic concept that asks, "If we were not now in this business, knowing what we now know, would we get into it?" If the answer is that, *knowing what we now know*, we would not start it up again today, then the next decision is, *how do you get out and how fast?*

One of the places where you continually apply zero-based thinking is with regard to people. "Knowing what we now know about this person, would we hire him or her? Knowing what we now know about this person's capabilities, would we put them in that position?" And if the answer is *no*, then the next question is, "How do we get rid of this person, or how do we redeploy this person?"

It takes courage to apply zero-based thinking to every part of your business on a regular basis, but avoiding it can lead to underachievement and failure. It can lead to inaction, passivity, and indecisiveness. Failure in business revolves around these key reasons, just as defeat in warfare is inextricably linked to them.

Investment and Divestment Strategy

Investment strategy asks where we put our resources to achieve the greatest return on investment. Where are we going to invest our resources in new product development, in technology, people, skill training, time commitment, and so on?

These questions also require that you consider your *divestment* strategy. What are you going to get out of, cut back on, remove, or eliminate? Divestment strategy means that you have to get rid of *yesterday* before you can go on to tomorrow.

One of the basic rules for resource allocation is for you to never get into something new until you get out of or discontinue something old. Your key resources are the time and talents of your executives. If you expand into new areas of activity and continue in old areas of activity, you will diffuse your efforts and your powers. You will simply not have enough resources to do everything well.

Perhaps the number one reason for the failure of businesses is investments in managerial ego, which takes place when you dig in concerning a product or service that is not selling or not succeeding. Investments in managerial ego lead companies to take their best salespeople, their best marketing people, and their advertising budgets and focus them on the products of yesterday rather than the opportunities of tomorrow.

Crisis Anticipation

This military term, *crisis anticipation*, is also relevant to business. Always be asking yourself, "What is the worst possible thing that could happen in this business in the months and years ahead?" Look down the road six months and 12 months and ask, "What could happen that could endanger or threaten the survival of our business?"

Then ask yourself what you would do, what actions would you take, if such a thing were to occur? How would you react or respond if you experienced a major setback or failure in your business? A key part of the leader's job is to look into the future and anticipate crises. It is to plan for the worst, should it occur. Your job is to always have a backup plan.

Choose Your Competition

Choosing your strategy means choosing your *competitor*. Who is your competitor? What is your competitor? What other companies or factors in your world determine your success or failure in your industry? Your competitors determine your level of sales, your profitability, your pricing, and how fast or how slow you grow. Establish who your competitors are and then ask yourself, "What do we have to do to win against determined competition in our market? What are our strengths and weaknesses relative to our competitors? What do we have to do to please our customers better than anyone else?"

Four Important Strategic Questions

The first key question in strategy is, "What is our business?"

What is your business today? Describe it clearly. Most people are not exactly clear what their business actually is. A good example is the history of railroads. The railroads used to think that their business was simply building and maintaining railroads, when their business was actually transporting goods and services.

Most of the railroads in the United States went bankrupt or nearly so because most of their transportation services were taken over by trucking, airplanes, and ships. In Canada, Canadian Pacific (CP) is a railroad, but it's also CP airlines, CP trucking, and CP shipping. Early on, CP determined that its business was the transportation of people and products, and it invested in every area of transporting people and products.

The second question is "What will it be?" If you don't do anything about your business today, knowing everything you know, what will it be in one or two or three years? How is your business changing? What will your customers want in two or three years that is different from today? What are the trends in your market?

Question number three is "What could it be?" What are the possibilities for your business? What are your best opportunities for the future? This question can open up a tremendous number of exciting possibilities.

A fourth question is "What should it be?" If you could wave a magic wand and make your business ideal in every way, how would it be different from today? What would it look like? What would you be doing? What kind of products or services would you offer? What levels of sales and profitability would you achieve? What kind of reputation would you have?

In strategic planning, one of the most important things that you do is to create a dream or vision of something that your business could be that is far greater and more exciting than it is doing today. Could you be a world leader in a particular product or service? Could you be the best in a particular area? Could you produce a product or service that people could say proudly: "This is the best product or service of its kind available anywhere"?

Could you create a corporate environment that is the most dynamic and innovative in your industry? Could you create a business that you could look at and say, "This is a great business"?

Continually ask yourself these four questions: (1) What is our business, defined in terms of how we take care of our customers? (2) What will it be, based on current trends? (3) What could our business be, if we made the necessary changes? and (4) What should it be, especially if we have no limitations?

Determine the Financial Objectives of Strategy

Financial objectives are the reason for setting strategy. Financial objectives and the changes in financial results are the key ways that you measure whether your strategy is effective. The first financial objective is *return on equity*, or the return on the actual amount of money working in the company, the amount invested and owned by the shareholders.

The next consideration is *return on investment*. It is the return on the actual amount of capital—your own investment, plus the money that you have borrowed from banks and other sources.

The third financial objective is *return on sales*. How much do you earn in net and gross profit for every dollar of sales?

The fourth number is *net profit*. In the final analysis, net profit is the only real measure of how well you're doing strategically. Net profits that increase consistently over time offer the proof that your business strategy is a good one. In the final analysis, every successful strategy leads to increased net profit. Net profit equals, in military terms, *victory*. It is net profit, or *free cash flow*, that enables the company to grow.

Set Strategies for Profitability

In the Profit Implications of Marketing Strategy (PIMS) studies, one of the most exhaustive studies done on what contributes to profitability, the researchers discovered two key factors that were most responsible for business profitability. The first discovery was the centrality of the *quality* of the product or service. It turns out to be the most important factor in business success. Striving for top quality and continually improving your product or service offerings provide the *offensive strategy* in business. Quality is a key profitability strategy. The quality leaders in every business are also the most profitable in their industries.

The second discovery of the PIMS studies was the importance of the *associated services* that accompanied the product or service offering. These factors include how the product is sold, serviced, delivered, packaged, and every aspect of how the customer is treated personally before, during, and after the purchase.

Define Quality

Quality is always defined and determined by your customer, your competitor, and by the alternatives that are available in the market place. Ask your customers. How do they define quality? What does quality mean to them? What do they seek when they are thinking of buying your product or service?

The answer is that it's not what you produce; rather, it is what they want. Many companies have no idea why customers buy their products. Many companies are not aware of why they are successful when they are, or unsuccessful when they are not. However, as Tom Peters says, the most successful companies are the ones with an internal mindset that is exactly the same as the customer's. They see the product or service the way the customer sees the product or service, and are continually working to increase the quality of the product or service relative to the *customer's* perception.

A key part of strategy and profitability is to make sure that your product or service is exactly what your customer needs, wants, and is willing to pay for.

Practice the Strategy of Quality Leadership

Begin by defining quality clearly, and make sure that everybody in your company can recognize quality when they see it. Make sure that each person knows what constitutes quality work and quality products or services. Be sure that everyone has a quality target to aim at, and that each job in the company can be measured.

The most profitable companies in the United States, and around the world today, are companies that have continuous internal and external focus on quality. Everyone talks about it, thinks about it, and continually works to improve it.

Action Exercises

1. Determine your exact goals and objectives in terms of sales, profitability, growth, and market share for the next 3–5 years.
2. Identify your driving force and resolve to put all your energies and resources into dominating your market in that area.
3. Mass and concentrate your resources, especially the people, products, services, and areas of excellence where you can attain market leadership.
4. Go on the offensive and resolve to move aggressively to take advantage of market opportunities, to sell more of your products and services in every way possible.
5. Practice zero-based thinking in every area; what are you doing today that, knowing what you now know, you wouldn't get into if you had it to do over?
6. Implement an ongoing investment and divestment strategy in your business, with your time, money, and resources. What should you get into, or out of?
7. Identify your competitive advantages in every area of your business, and continually seek ways to offer your products and services better, faster, cheaper, and more conveniently to your customers.

CHAPTER 3

THE DISCIPLINE
OF CONTROL

"There is but one use of power, and that is to serve people."

—George H. W. Bush

The discipline of control, of self-control and self-responsibility, is the true mark of the leader and of the exceptional person in every area. The fact is that you feel *positive* about yourself to the degree to which you feel in control of yourself and of your life. You feel negative about yourself, and stressed in your work when you feel you are not in control, or that you are controlled by other people or circumstances. Psychologists refer to this "sense of control" as what happens when you feel largely able to handle what happens to you.

Various international surveys measure the percentage of the population that feels in control of their lives, as opposed to feeling that they are largely controlled by government, culture, or society. For example, in the United States, fully 68 percent of the population feels that they exert a lot or total control over what happens to them. In Germany by contrast, only 32 percent of the population feel that they have any real control over their lives.

Control and Personal Freedom

A direct relationship connects how much you feel *in control* with your level of happiness and personal freedom. This element of personal control has been researched extensively over the years. Its psychological definition is "locus of control theory."

It seems that each person has a *locus*, or place, of control, which determines how much the person feels that he or she controls their life, work, and family. A person with an "internal locus of control" feels very much in charge of his or her life and what happens to him or her. Such a person decides what he or she does or doesn't do, rather than feeling obligated to do what others want or expect.

On the other hand, a person with an "external locus of control" does not feel in control or is out of control. This person feels little power to shape his or her own life, but rather feels controlled by a boss, bills, personal problems, health, society, and other factors.

People with an internal locus of control are more proactive, creative, outgoing, and self-confident. They are the men and women who become leaders in every area. People with an external locus of control are more passive, unsure, indecisive, and more prone to stress, negativity, and anger. Your goal is to develop an internal locus of control and to become a powerful, confident, take-charge executive, in control of yourself, your environment, and others.

Responsibility and Control

The central issue in leadership and feelings of control is the concept of responsibility.

People can be organized on a scale from 1 to 10 based on how much responsibility they accept for their lives, and in how many different areas. Those who score 10 accept 100 percent responsibility for their lives and for everything that happens to them. Those who score 1 accept no responsibility for themselves or their situations, and blame everything that happens to them on other people, the past, or outside factors. Everyone is located somewhere on this scale, moving up or down based on each decision made.

It is not possible to imagine an effective leader who dodges and evades responsibility, although among managers and lower-level employees it sometimes occurs.

A direct relationship is evident between the acceptance of responsibility and a feeling of control. Further, a direct relationship can be traced between a sense of control, the acceptance of responsibility, and *happiness*. This direct relationship also extends from a sense of control, responsibility, happiness on to a sense of optimism and personal power.

The Irresponsible Attitude

The opposite of accepting responsibility is an attitude of irresponsibility. Irresponsible people manifest this attitude in four ways:

1. They continually *make excuses* when they fail to perform. They see themselves as victims and are often saying the equivalent of "It's not my fault."
2. They *complain* continually about people and circumstances. They see themselves as victims of things that have happened.
3. They *criticize* other people on a regular basis, usually behind their backs, and tend to gossip regularly about people in a negative way.
4. Worst of all, irresponsible people *blame others* continually, past and present, for all their problems. They are never at fault. They are never responsible.

The Qualities of the Leader

The mark of a leader is that he or she accepts complete responsibility for the situation:

1. A leader never makes *excuses* if things go wrong or if he or she drops the ball occasionally. Instead a leader says, "No excuses. I did it, or I didn't do it, but I have no excuses."
2. A leader doesn't *complain* about people or situations, which is basically a sign of weakness. When a leader is not happy with the situation, he or she does something about it and takes action. If

the leader can't take action, he or she accepts the situation and moves on.

3. A leader does not *criticize* others. If someone makes a mistake, the leader discusses it with that person, agrees on a course of action, and gets back to work.

4. Especially, a leader does not *blame* other people or circumstances for the current situation. Instead, leaders accept responsibility and get busy doing something to fix the problem. As Harry Truman so famously said, "The buck stops here."

Perhaps the most powerful words you can use to take full control of your emotions and the situation are the words, "I am responsible." The minute you say "I am responsible," you are back in charge. When you say "I am responsible," you become calm, clear, and positive once more.

The Key to High Performance

Perhaps the biggest threats to health, happiness, and high performance are negative emotions of all kinds. Negative emotions are the primary source of most of our unhappiness in life and work.

You can eliminate negative emotions by using the power of your mind. Because your mind can only hold one thought at a time, positive or negative, you can deliberately choose to substitute a positive thought for a negative thought. As soon as you affirm the words, "I am responsible," your negative emotions stop, like switching off a light. It is not possible to say "I am responsible" and remain negative. These powerful words cancel the negative feeling immediately. Whenever something negative or unfortunate happens, the words "I am responsible" put you in complete control of your emotions. "I am responsible" moves you into high-performance mode. They are the words of a leader.

Taking Control

How do you take complete control over yourself, your emotions, and the quality of your thinking? You begin by going over each part of your life, like examining an inventory sheet, and then accepting 100 percent responsibility for every person or situation in your life that causes you any negativity or aggravation. Instead of using your mind to think of reasons why other people are at fault, you use your wonderful powers of reasoning to determine why and how you may personally be responsible, even partially, for the negative situation. And these reasons can always be found.

One of the most common examples of this way of thinking is when a manager complains about the poor performance of a staff member. As soon as you ask the questions about who *hired* the person, who placed the person in that position, who assigned a particular responsibility to that person, and who is in charge of managing, motivating, and disciplining that person, it becomes immediately clear that it is the manager who is at fault, not the employee.

Build the Discipline of Responsibility in Others

Once you have developed the discipline of taking complete responsibility for yourself, you then teach this to others. The fastest way to build confidence and competence in people is to give them more responsibility. You grow them by giving them freedom to perform, and then by supporting and encouraging them when they make a mistake.

Your goal as a leader is to be a role model of personal responsibility, and then to encourage everyone else to accept higher levels of responsibility themselves. Continually tell people, "You are responsible," and then help them to take charge of their decisions and actions. The essence of self-control is self-responsibility. Responsibility and control are essential to high performance in management and in leadership.

In business, it seems that the people who experience the highest levels of stress are middle management. The people above them, the senior executives, feel a high level of control over their decisions and actions. The people below the middle managers, their staff and employees, feel a low burden of responsibility for results. It is the middle managers who are controlled by their bosses, who exert only a limited control over their staff, and who are expected to perform and get results regardless, and consequently, they are the ones who experience the greatest amount of stress in the world of work.

Your goal as a leader is to take complete control over yourself, your emotions, and your work. You increase your sense of control by developing the habit of automatically accepting responsibility for your life and your situation. Even if something negative has happened that has nothing to do with you, you are still responsible for the way you react and respond to the situation.

Action Exercises

1. Identify the areas of your life and work where you feel the greatest sense of control.
2. Identify those areas of your life where you feel that you have little or no control, where you feel that you are controlled by other people or circumstances.
3. Resolve today to accept 100 percent responsibility for every part of your life; think about how and why you are responsible for your situation and for everything that happens to you.
4. Refuse to criticize, complain, or blame others for anything. You are the leader. You are in charge.
5. Set an example by telling others that you are responsible when things go wrong, rather than making excuses.
6. Encourage others to accept greater responsibility for their actions and for getting results in their work.
7. Give people who accept responsibility considerable freedom to do their work and encourage them when they make mistakes.

CHAPTER FOUR

THE DISCIPLINE
OF CHARACTER

"In the long run, the best proof of character is good actions."

—John Stuart Mill

A chief responsibility of leadership is to be an example to others—a role model whom others can look up to. Being a role model has everything to do with personality and character: personality is how you behave, but character is what you are. Character is what you do when no one is looking. All great men and women are recognized for the quality of their character.

It was said that the character of George Washington was the foundation upon which the American Revolution and Republic were built. After his death, he was called "the indispensable man." Even to this day, it is commonly believed that the United States would not have come into existence if not for the incredible strength of character of Washington from the beginning of the revolution through to his stepping down voluntarily at the end of his second term.

The Quality of Integrity

The foundation of character is the quality of integrity. Integrity means honesty toward others; always telling the truth. Integrity also means a commitment to quality performance in everything you do, as an expression of the person you really are inside. Integrity means that you live in truth with others, and that you live in truth with yourself. You never say or do anything that you feel to be untrue. Having integrity also means that you never stay in or tolerate a situation that requires you to compromise your innermost values and principles. No matter what it costs, you speak out or get up and walk away.

How can you tell who a person really is inside? How can you determine his or her beliefs, goals, and values? Is it is what he or she says, writes, or declares when running for public office? No, it is what a person actually *does* that shows the real truth about that person. Only action is truth, especially action under pressure. In Peter Drucker's words, "Leadership is action, not position."

The Power of Choice

Humans are "choosing organisms." People make choices continually, hundreds of them every day. Every choice, however, implies a *rejection* of all other choices that you could make at that moment. You cannot do two things at the same time. Every choice, therefore, is a true expression of what you value more and what you value less at that moment.

You can discern the truth about a person by observing that person's behaviors and choices, especially under pressure, when forced to choose one way or another. You develop a quality or discipline by making a decision to practice that quality, especially integrity, at all times and under all circumstances.

Determine Your Values

Start with your values, your most important choices. What are the three to five most important values or principles that you live by? Be honest with yourself. Determine what is really important to you personally, rather than what might sound good or what might be important to someone else.

Most values are hardwired from an early age as the result of an individual's upbringing and formative experiences. They seldom change.

People at the age of 47 or 48 are much like the people they were at the age of 17 or 18. Basic personality remains consistent over time.

A true value is always accompanied by an *emotion*. A value triggers deep feelings when that value is discussed or demonstrated. You always love and admire in another person those values that you most admire and respect in yourself, or in anyone else. Your best friends will always be people with whom you share the same values.

What you like and enjoy, what moves you emotionally, whether it is in other people, art, movies, literature, or poetry, is an expression of what you really believe in and care about—your innermost values and convictions. When you enjoy a movie or a book where the qualities of courage and determination are demonstrated, you are showing that you strongly relate to these values; they are values you admire and to which you aspire.

Buy In or Not Buy In

Jack Welch, when he was president of General Electric, wrote that there were two kinds of people in the business: those who *bought in* to the company's values and those who did *not buy in*. He said that most of the problems in business come from those people who were competent in their work, good at their jobs, but who did not buy in to the values of General Electric. This insight turns out to be the same in any business.

When Thomas J. Watson Jr. founded IBM in the 1920s, he set out the company's values in the book *A Business and Its Beliefs*. IBM was founded and built on specific values from the very beginning: *respect for the individual, the best customer service, and superior accomplishment of all tasks*. For the rest of the twentieth century, these values were inviolable at IBM. Did they have an influence on business results? Partially because of its passionate commitment to these values, by 1980, IBM had more than 80 percent of the world computer market. *Fortune* regularly rated IBM as the most admired company in America, if not the world. IBM's customers and personnel were loyal to the company to a degree seldom seen in the business world.

Today, every greatly admired company is known for its values. They could be quality (Lexus, Mercedes, Rolex), innovation (Apple, Google, Samsung), customer service (Nordstrom, FedEx, Enterprise Rent-a-Car), or people—a commitment to creating a great place to work.

Define Your Values

The starting point of character for yourself and your business is to determine the values you love, respect, and aspire to, and to define what each of these values means *in action*. For example, your personal value could be integrity. You could make this value actionable by saying "Integrity means that I am honest with myself and others; I always tell the truth and I keep my word." This statement gives you a measure and a mental track to run on. You can use this definition to guide your choices and behaviors whenever you have to choose between two courses of action. Of course, if you always keep your word and fulfill your promises, it is wise to give your word carefully and sparingly, taking time to think about the situation and the likely consequences before you commit.

If your company value is "excellent customer service," like Enterprise Rent-a-Car, this value would mean that everybody in the company gives superior customer service at all times, under all conditions. The customer is King, or Queen.

The president of a large oil company once interrupted a strategic planning session where integrity was being discussed as a value by the executive team. He said these profound words: "It seems to me that integrity is not a value in itself; it is instead the value that guarantees all the others." Truer words were never spoken. Your level of integrity is the measure by which you live up to your other values, especially when it costs you time and money.

Practice Your Values

Think of the passengers on Flight 93 headed toward the Pentagon or White House, who stood up, knowing they were going to die, and followed Todd Beemer when he said, "Let's roll!" Those individuals believed in the values of courage, self-responsibility, and patriotism, and they demonstrated their commitment to these values by dying for them in that field in Pennsylvania.

Your adherence to what you say you believe in, your actions minute by minute, tell yourself and everyone else who you really are. Consider that it is said your children will ignore or forget the words you say, but will be permanently shaped by the things you do and the example you set. Therefore, it is important that, as a leader in your company, you lead and shape the behaviors of others by the example you set.

Return to Values

Here is an interesting discovery: almost all problems can be resolved by a return to values. In my book, *The Power of Self-Confidence*, I report on the seemingly direct relationship between living in truth, consistent with your values on the one hand, and the wonderful feelings of self-esteem and self-confidence you enjoy on the other hand. When you set high standards for yourself and your business, and insist on living up to them, no matter what the cost, you feel terrific about yourself, and so does everyone else.

Saint Francis of Assisi made two profound observations. First, he said, "You are not punished *for* your sins, but *by* them." The second statement attributed to him was, "It's heaven all the way to heaven, and it's hell all the way to hell." You are immediately, emotionally, and spiritually rewarded when you live by your values and principles. It's heaven all the way to heaven when you live and practice the things you really believe. And because nature is balanced and fair, the opposite seems to be true as well.

Practice Self-Mastery and Self-Control

Character means many other things as well. Character requires the self-mastery, self-control, and self-discipline of delayed gratification. Character means that you never seek out something for nothing, easy money, or quick riches. Character requires that you are willing to suffer "short-term pain for long-term gain," rather than the more common practice of "short-term gain for long-term pain."

Many years ago, a wise businessman, Albert Grey, after 13 years of study, concluded that "successful people were those who made a habit of doing the things that failures didn't like to do." And what were those things that failures didn't like to do? Well, they turned out to be the same things that successful people didn't like to do either, but successful people did them anyway because they knew they were part of the price of success.

Denis Waitley said, "Successful people do what is goal-achieving; failures do what is stress-relieving." The good news is that character is like any discipline. The more you practice it, the sooner it becomes a permanent part of your personality. Consider the following saying:

"Sow a thought and you reap an action;
Sow an act and you reap a habit;
Sow a habit and you reap a character;
Sow a character and you reap a destiny."

Fortunately, you are always *free to choose*. Your character today is the sum total of all your past choices and decisions. You can change your future because you can choose to change your actions today. You can make new choices and better decisions.

You can become an exemplary leader and an excellent person by simply going to work on yourself, by committing to live in truth and demonstrating character in everything you do, with everyone you meet.

Action Exercises

1. Select three to five values that are most important to you, write them down, and create a statement that describes how you will practice them each day.

2. As a leader in your business, either decide your operational values and share them with your staff, or bring your staff together to discuss and agree the values you will practice together.

3. Identify those occasions where you have adhered to higher values in dealing with problems in your business in the past. What did you learn?

4. Identify those areas where you failed to live up to your values. What happened?

5. Share your values with everyone in your company, and with your customers, perhaps on your website. Making them public is a real motivation for sticking to your values in the future.

6. Decide what kind of a reputation you want to have with your customers. What words do you want them to use when they describe you to others?

7. Identify three things you could do immediately to make yourself and your company more values-based.

CHAPTER FIVE

THE DISCIPLINE OF COMPETENCE

"Leaders are people we as followers want to regard with awe as the fullest flowering of our own possibilities."

—Gail Sheehy

Top leaders and successful people in every area of life are those who have committed to excellence in their chosen fields. They have developed the discipline of always doing a good job, no matter how much longer it takes, or how difficult it turns out to be. The payoff is that happy, successful people are recognized as very good at what they do.

Perhaps the most important part of your personality, and the foundation of your happiness, is determined by your level of self-esteem. Your self-esteem is defined as "how much you like yourself." It is how much you consider yourself to be valuable and important that determines the quality of your inner life. The more you like yourself, the more confidence you have. The more you like yourself, the more you will like others, and the more they will like you and be open to being influenced by you. The more you like yourself, the bigger goals you will set, and the more you will persist in the achievement of those goals.

Your level of self-esteem is the control valve on your performance. It determines how happy and effective you are in every part of your life.

The Roots of Low Self-Esteem

Many people, as the result of destructive criticism and a lack of unconditional love in childhood, grow up with low levels of self-esteem and self-confidence. These deficits hurt their happiness and performance in adult life. Louise Hay wrote, "The root of most unhappiness is the feeling that 'I'm not good enough.'" It is deep feelings of inadequacy and inferiority that hold people back more than any other factors.

Fortunately, the flipside to this inadequacy on the coin of self-esteem is called "self-efficacy," or how competent and capable you feel you are in a particular area. The good news is that the better you become at any skill, the more you like yourself. And the more you like yourself, the better you perform and the more effective or *efficacious* you become at whatever you do.

Resolve to Be the Best

One of the most important decisions you make in your career is to "be the best" at what you do. Resolve to do your work in an excellent fashion. Decide today to be in the top 10 percent in your industry, both personally and in your business.

When I was in my twenties, an older executive told me one day about the 80/20 rule. He said that the top 20 percent of people in any field earn 80 percent of the money in that field. I had never heard this "Pareto Principle" before. The idea both encouraged and discouraged me. It encouraged me because it was motivational and aspirational. It made me want to get into the top 20 percent myself. But this revelation also discouraged me. I had not graduated from high school and had worked at laboring jobs for several years. I had never really been very good at anything.

Then I learned two things that changed my life. First, I learned that everyone in the top 20 percent had started in the bottom 20 percent. I learned that everyone who is good in any field was once poor in that field.

The second thing I learned was that all business skills are *learnable*. You can learn any skill you need to learn to achieve any business goal you can set for yourself or your company. No limits. Remember, leaders are made and not born. And they are self-made, through work on themselves, through personal development. Your job is to set excellence in your field as your goal, and then to work toward it until you achieve it.

Here is another discovery: anything less than a commitment to excellence is an acceptance of *mediocrity*. It seems that mediocrity—being in the bottom 80 percent of people or companies in any field—is the "default setting" on most individuals and organizations. Mediocre performance takes place *automatically* in the absence of a 100 percent do-or-die commitment to excellent performance of your work.

Leaders Commit to Excellence

One of the greatest motivators in the world of work is the commitment to excellence by the top people in any organization. Companies that are recognized as quality leaders in their fields attract and keep the best people. Excellent companies have high morale. People like to brag that they work for a company that is known for excellent products and excellent services.

As the leader, getting everyone to commit to excellence, as well as leading by your own example of excellent work habits, is one of the most powerful and important contributions you can make. The starting point in developing the discipline of competence, of excellence, is for you to select the specific areas and tasks where excellence is most important in generating higher sales and profitability.

Fortunately, determining this starting point is not complicated. You can break each job, including your own, down into about five to seven key result areas, seldom more. You can then give yourself a grade of 1 to 10 in each area to determine how good you or others are at the most important things you do. Evaluating where you are is the starting point of personal and business improvement.

The admission of weakness in a key result area is actually a sign of strength. It is only when you can admit that you are not sufficiently good in a particular skill area that you can begin to improve in that area. It is only then that you can learn how to make the most valuable contribution possible to your business. It is only when you admit that you could be better that you can learn and grow toward the fulfillment of your true potential.

Learn New Skills, Improve the Old

Peter Drucker wrote, "The only skill that will be important in the twenty-first century will be the skill of learning new skills. All else will eventually become obsolete."

In their book, *Competing for the Future,* Gary Hamel and C. K. Prahalad pointed out that every business is built on *core competencies,* as is the career of every executive. They defined *core competency* as a skill that the individual or organization did especially well in comparison to others and was essential to the success of the business. The key question they asked was, "What core competencies in skill and execution will you have to have in five years to be a leader in your industry?"

Whatever your answer to that question, you should begin immediately to develop, hire, or buy these competencies before your competitors do.

Strive for Personal Excellence

Striving for excellence is necessary for both the company and for you as an individual. Core competencies are the foundation of business success and of business and personal excellence. The axiom today is, "Whatever got you to where you are today is not enough to keep you there." Whatever the reasons for your success today, you will have to be doing things much better one year from now if you want to survive, much less grow in your industry.

Start with yourself. Ask the key question that can most help you move ahead: "What one skill, if I was absolutely excellent at it, consistently, would enable me to make the greatest possible contribution to my business?" Ask this question of yourself regularly. Encourage each person who reports to you to ask and answer this question. Then ask it of your company overall: "What one skill or competence, if we were absolutely excellent at it, would most help us increase our sales and profitability?"

"Our only real competitive advantage is our ability to learn and apply new skills faster than our competitors."
—quotation from a top executive

"Excellence is not a destination; it is a way of life."
—Aristotle

"The quality of your life will be determined by your commitment to excellence, regardless of your chosen field."
—Vince Lombardi

Resolve today to be the best at what you do personally, and then resolve to be the best in every area of the business that is important to your customers. Nothing will be more effective in helping you to rise to the top of your field and to become an excellent leader than for you to develop a reputation for excellence in everything you do.

Continuous Learning Opens Every Door

The key to the development of competence is continuous learning: your commitment to keeping current in your field, and devoting time every day, every week, to maintaining and upgrading your knowledge and skills. A simple three-part formula can help you get on top and stay ahead of the other people in your field. It involves reading, listening, and taking additional courses and training.

Read Daily

First, make a decision to read in your chosen field for 30 to 60 minutes each day, preferably in the morning. It is said that *reading is to the mind as exercise is to the body.* By reading 30–60 minutes each day, along with underlining and making notes while thinking of how you might use this new information, you actually strengthen your mind and increase your intelligence. Reading one book per month will put you in the top 1 percent of business people working today. Reading 30–60 minutes per day will translate into about one book per week, or about 50 books per year. To earn a PhD at a leading university requires that you read and synthesize the content of 30 to 50 books, which means that reading 30–60 minutes each day actually earns for you the equivalent of a PhD in your field each year.

Here is a question: Do you think that by continually upgrading your skills in this manner, by earning the equivalent of a PhD each year, you would greatly affect your ability to get results and improve your income?

Over the years, I have given this advice to many thousands of people. Without exception, the people who take this advice come back and tell me that it has transformed their lives. They have gone from rags to riches; from junior employees to presidents of their organizations; or from struggling to great financial success by the simple exercise of reading and learning and growing each and every day throughout their careers.

Listen to Educational Audio Programs

The second part of continuous learning is for you to listen to educational audio programs as you move around. Instead of listening to music as many people do, download audio courses produced by experts in your field and listen to them whenever you have spare moments. For many years I advocated listening to audio programs in your car, and I still do. But today, most people listen to audio on their iPhones or MP3 players, and you can do the same. According to the University of Southern California, by listening to educational audio programs as you drive from place to place, you can get the educational equivalent of almost full-time attendance at the university.

An even greater benefit comes from audio learning, however. When you take an academic course at a university, most of what you learn is theoretical and difficult to apply to the real world. When you listen to an audio program, much of what you hear on the recording is proven, practical, and immediately actionable. And if it is not, you either jump forward in the program or discontinue it altogether. You don't waste a minute learning anything you cannot use immediately to improve your life or work.

Take Seminars and Workshops

The third area in which you can engage in continuous learning is attending seminars and workshops given by experts in your field. You can learn more in one or two days from an expert than you might learn by yourself in 10 or 20 years, if at all. Jim Rohn said, "It's not the cost of the book or the course that counts, it's the cost of not having that information that you must consider."

Deliberate Practice

In Geoff Colvin's best-selling book *Talent Is Overrated* (2010), he reports on the research studying the people who eventually got to the top of *Fortune* 500 corporations. The researchers began by assuming that these *superstars* were people who, from an early age, were clearly more intelligent and ambitious than the average person.

What they found was quite the contrary. Everyone seems to start off very much the same at the beginning of their working lifetime. But the people who got to the top of their fields used a method that the researchers called "deliberate practice." At each stage of their careers, they would identify the *one skill* that could help them the most at that time; they would then focus single-mindedly on developing that skill. They would read the books, listen to the audio programs, and take the courses necessary to master that skill. They would keep working in this area until people started to compliment them on how good they were. At this stage they would then move on to the development of the next skill that could help them the most at that time. They did not try to learn 100 things at once. They learned their craft of management and leadership one skill at a time. And you can do the same.

Continually ask yourself, "What one skill, if I was absolutely excellent at it, consistently, would enable me to make the greatest contribution to my company?" If you don't know the answer to this question, go and ask your boss. Ask your coworkers. Ask your friends and mentors. But you must know the answer, and you must be working on it all the time until you master that skill.

One Skill Away

Sometimes you may be only one skill from a major breakthrough in your career. Sometimes you may be only one skill away from dramatically improving the quality of your life, your work, and your business. Earl Nightingale said, "Success is the progressive realization of a worthy goal or ideal."

When you set a goal to become excellent in a particular skill area, and you begin working toward that goal each day; as you experience success, you experience a continuous feeling of happiness and personal growth. The very act of learning becomes self-motivating. It makes you happy.

Nido Qubein, president of High Point University, says that, "It is competence that leads to confidence." The better you feel you are at doing your job, the greater your sense of forward motion, and the more positive and confident you become to apply your skills to get even better results.

Leaders are learners. They never stop learning and growing in their fields. They are hungry for new information. They are ambitious to become excellent at what they do. Continuous learning is the foundation of competence, both as a person and as a leader.

Action Exercises

1. Make a decision today to dedicate yourself to lifelong learning. Work on yourself as if your future depended on it, because it does.

2. Identify the one skill that, if you were absolutely excellent at it, would most help you in your current position, and make a plan to develop that skill.

3. Ask successful people around you for recommendations for the best business books they have read recently, and then either buy, order, or download that book immediately.

4. Set aside a certain time each day to read, study, and upgrade your knowledge and skill in your field, then discipline yourself to do it each day.

5. Encourage your staff to identify the key skill areas where they need to learn and grow, and then provide the time and resources they need to develop those skills.

6. Listen to educational audio programs rather than music from now on; download them onto your smartphone so you have them instantly available.

7. Resolve to attend two or more seminars or workshops on key subjects in your field each year. Then apply what you learn immediately when you return.

CHAPTER SIX

THE DISCIPLINE OF COMPETITIVENESS

"You must conquer and rule or lose and serve,
triumph or suffer, be the hammer or the anvil."
—Goethe

The primary reason for the success or failure of a business, according to Dun and Bradstreet, is the success or failure of the marketing effort. Forty-eight percent of all business failures can be attributed to a slowing down or ineffectiveness in the area of marketing and sales. In our dynamic, competitive economy, marketing is the core function of every successful enterprise.

Strategic marketing is the art and science of determining what your customers and future customers really want, need, can use, and afford—and then of helping them to get it by creating and structuring your products and services in such a way that they satisfy the specific needs of the customers you have identified. The goal of strategic marketing is to enable you to sell more of your offerings at higher prices over an extended geographical area, and achieve market stability, strength, and leadership.

The starting point of successful marketing is to remember that customers are always right. They buy for their reason, not yours. Customers are selfish, demanding, ruthless, disloyal, and fickle. But they are always right from their own rationale. They will change suppliers whenever they perceive that they will be better served elsewhere. Your ability to appeal to their real desires and to satisfy their wants and needs as they perceive them determines your success in business.

Marketing is a skill set that can and must be learned by keeping certain key ideas and concepts in mind continually, and by asking certain vital questions regularly. If you take the time to think through the answers to the questions in this program, you will sharpen your marketing skills considerably.

The Purpose of a Business

The purpose of a business is not to make a profit. The purpose is to create and keep a customer. All the efforts of a successful business are aimed at creating customers. Profits are the *result* of creating and keeping customers in a cost-effective way.

The cost of creating customers initially is high. The cost of keeping them is far lower than that of creating them. The most successful companies are the best at marketing. Their strategies are all aimed at creating and keeping more customers.

The first key to strategic marketing is quality. It is the most powerful of all marketing strategies. People will always come back to a quality supplier of goods and services.

The second key to strategic marketing is excellent customer service. Quality products combined with superb service, in comparison with your competitors, are the primary factors that determine market success.

The purpose of marketing is to create perceptions of *unique added value* in your products and services in comparison with your competitors. The aim of marketing is to differentiate your company, your products, and your services—in the minds of your customers—from those of your competitors. No product or service offering occurs separate and apart from the market, from what else is available to the same customer for the same amount of money.

Four Approaches to Successful Marketing

You can approach the market with your products and services in four ways. The first is by creating *utility* in satisfying the needs of your customers. You offer something they need and can use to accomplish their other goals. A perfect example is a shovel or a truck, each of which has useful utility value. An example of a new industry that was built on utility values or needs is FedEx. FedEx created an industry that had never existed before when founder Fred Smith saw a growing need for rapid letter and package delivery, preferably overnight, because of the slowness of regular mail.

A second approach is *pricing*: You can create new markets by bringing your goods and services into the price range of your customers. How could you price your products or services so that more customers could afford to buy them? Many companies have been able to achieve market leadership by focusing on pricing. The greater your market share and the lower your cost of production, the lower will be the prices you can charge. The Japanese have used this strategy brilliantly. They price their products low initially to gain market share. As sales volume increases, they achieve economies of scale in manufacturing. They then pass their lower costs on to the customer in the form of lower prices, and again, increased their market share.

Walmart has used this strategy of lowering costs via volume purchasing, passing the savings on to its customers, which leads to greater sales volume and the ability to pass even greater savings on to its customers. By combining lower prices with efficient distribution, Walmart has become the most successful retailer in the world. How might you apply this strategy to your business?

Henry Ford's Insight

Henry Ford's strategy is a perfect example of pricing strategy. His objective with mass production was to get the cost of an automobile within the price range of the average American family. His success enabled him to become one of the richest men of his time. At one time Ford had 60 percent of the U.S. automobile market, a record never achieved before or since.

The third marketing strategy is adapting to the customer's reality, both social and economic. A perfect example is Sears when it became the world's largest retailer by initiating an unconditional money back guarantee policy when the company was in the catalog business. The customers' reality up until that time was that if they bought something from the catalog that didn't work or didn't fit, they were stuck with it. Sears realized that the way to overcome that major barrier to purchasing was to adapt their product offerings to the customer's reality and the customer's needs. This change led to a revolution in merchandising and retail sales, with unconditional guarantees now the norm for almost all businesses.

The fourth approach to marketing strategy is to deliver what represents "true value" to the customer. True value can only be found by working closely with your customers. IBM is the perfect example. In the field of high-tech equipment, what represents true value is not only the ability to use it, but the assurance that it will be serviced if something fails. IBM provided the security that once you bought its products you were protected with service support if the equipment broke down.

Three Key Questions

First, is there a market? Will people out there actually buy the product or service you are thinking about bringing to the market? Remember that the basic ratio is 80/20, which means that 80 percent of all new products will fail. They will not achieve significant market share and the company will lose money and sometimes go out of business. Twenty percent will succeed in that they will pay their costs of investment and turn a profit. One of these 20 will be a star. The reality, then, is that of 100 new products introduced to the market in any given year, only one will be a runaway bestseller.

The next question in new product development is to ask: "Is the market *large* enough?" Too many businesspeople, especially entrepreneurs, fail to ask and answer this question before bringing a product to market. Can you sell enough of your product or service to make it economically worthwhile?

Thirdly, you must ask: "Is the market *concentrated* enough to approach economically?" Just because you can find people here and there who say they would buy your product or service, they offer no assurance that the market is concentrated enough for you to reach it with existing market methods or distribution channels. You may find that a market for 100,000 units of your product exists, but if that market is spread over all of North America in 10,000 cities, towns, and villages, how will you reach that market? A product or service that actually has a large market may not be feasible for you simply because you cannot reach that market in a cost-effective way, even with the Internet. The way you get your product or service from the company to your customer is often more important than the product itself.

Customer Analysis

When really looking at your potential customers, you need to ask several questions.

Question #1: "*Who* exactly is my customer?" You must ask this question, along with other more detailed questions to get the full answer. Who buys your product now? Who bought it in the past? Who is likely to buy it in the future? What is his/her age, education, income, tastes, attitudes, values, occupation, family structure, and so on? These answers form the starting point of all market research. If you can accurately identify your ideal customer, then designing the products and services, choosing the correct marketing channels, and selecting the best advertising and promotion to get to that customer become much easier. It is amazing how many companies start off with a product or service and don't know for sure exactly who is going to buy it. Who you think your customers are and who they actually turn out to be may be different too. For this reason, continuous market research is necessary.

Question #2: "*Why* does my customer buy my product or service?" What value does he/she seek? What change, improvement, outcome or result does your customer expect if he buys from you?

Question #3: "*Where* is my customer?" Geography is especially import to the where question. Are they urban or rural, in the wealthy neighborhoods or in the poor neighborhoods? Do they work for big companies or small companies? These answers will play a significant role in where you manufacture and your choice of marketing channels.

Question #4: "*How* does my customer buy?" Does your customer normally purchase your product through direct mail, wholesale, retail, or online? What is the buying process that your customer goes through before making a buying decision?

Question #5: "Why *don't* qualified customers buy from me?" Why do they buy from your competitors? What value do they see in buying from others that they don't see in your product or service? Why do they fail to buy at all, either from you or from your competitors?

Why People Buy

People buy products and services to satisfy needs, to solve problems, or to achieve specific goals. People buy products and services to improve their lives or work in some way. They buy to move from a state of lesser satisfaction to a state of greater satisfaction. No one will buy a product or service unless they feel they will experience an improvement in their conditions of some kind. Focusing your advertising and promotion on how the customer is going to be better off is the key to successful marketing.

One of the most important discoveries to come out of the Harvard research of Theodore Leavitt is that people buy the *feeling* that they anticipate enjoying as a result of owning or using the product or service. What feeling exactly will your customers experience when they buy your product or service?

Identify the Feeling

People buy for psychic satisfactions—the *emotional* content—far more often than for any other reason. You must determine how people are going to feel as a result of owning or using your product or service. Once you identify this "feeling," it becomes the core focus of all your marketing and sales activities. Quality, service, and especially the relationships you have with your customers are so important, because they generate the emotional component of any product or service in the mind of the customer. What do your customers anticipate feeling when they think about buying your product or service? Do you know? How can you create that feeling?

People in business will buy a product or service to *save* time or money, or to *earn* time or money. Time and money are almost interchangeable in terms of desirability in our society. Every appeal aimed at saving time or money likely creates a strong emotional pull for at least 90 percent of your target audience.

Two Basic Buying Needs

The two basic customer needs that trigger buying behavior are the desire for gain and the fear of loss. How does your product or service appeal to these needs? The more basic the need, the more simple and direct the appeal needs to be. If your product satisfies a safety, survival, or security need, such as a home security system or smoke alarm, then your appeal can be something like "Don't let your family die in the night. Install the system you need to protect them." If what you are selling is a complex or indirect need, like perfume or jewelry, then your market approach has to be much more subtle. "Be more beautiful, charming, and desirable to the most important person in your life."

Need analysis is vitally important. People need security, comfort, leisure, love, respect, and fulfillment—in that order of progression. Whatever you are selling you have to ask, "What need does this fill?" Answering this question is how you determine what kind of marketing appeal you are going to use.

Competitive Analysis

Competitive analysis is essential to effective marketing. It provides the starting point of differentiating your product or services from all the others.

Who are your competitors? Your competition determines how much you will sell; when you will sell it; and the size, quality, and your mix of service and relationships. Your competitors will determine whether you succeed or fail, how much profit you make on sales, and how much return you earn on your investment. Knowing your competitors is critical.

Who or what is *your* competition? Often you can identify a specific company or a series of companies that compete with you for the same customer. How can you present your product or service as being superior to your competitors?

The "what is my competition" question is just as important as the "who is my customer" question. Frequently the answer to the "what" question about your main competitor is market ignorance. Often your competition, the main factor stopping you from selling as much as you want, is that people don't know about your product or service, and how good it could be for them. It could be that what you really need is more public relations, market awareness, advertising, and promotion.

Why Do They Buy from Your Competition?

You need to thoroughly and honestly appraise the reasons why people buy from your competition. What benefit or advantage do customers see in buying from them rather than from you? What are the competition's strengths, and what could you do to offset those strengths?

Another part of competitive analysis requires that you ask, "Why should they switch?" Why should anybody stop buying from a competitor and switch to you? People don't switch just because you advertise, promote, and have a nice package. They switch because they are convinced that they will be better off buying from you than from buying from someone they already know.

Getting people to switch from a known source of product or service to an unknown source is especially difficult unless your competitive advantages are obvious and attractive. Competitive advantages—both yours and those of your competition—need to be thought out and described clearly.

Test Your Assumptions

What are your critical *assumptions* about your competition? Errant assumptions are at the root of most marketing failures. Could your assumptions about your competition be wrong? If they were wrong, what would have to change?

The biggest mistake frequently made with regard to competition is in failing to respect them enough. We underestimate their intelligence, tenacity, and their desire to drive us into the sea in pursuit of market share and profitability. Always assume that your competition is smart, competent, caring, intelligent, and thinking about the same things that you're considering. Don't ever underestimate them. Ask yourself, "What are they doing right?" Once you know what they are doing right, which is obtaining market share and sales, ask yourself how you could creatively imitate your competition in order to be better.

Achieving Competitive Advantage

The purpose of marketing is to create perceptions of unique added value in the minds of your customers. To survive and grow, every product and service offering must have some clear, distinct competitive advantage in comparison with competitive products or services that your potential customer could buy.

Achieving competitive advantage is the key to increased sales and higher profitability. It is absolutely essential that you are excellent at something that is important enough to your customers that they will pay money to obtain it. You have to be able to say to your customers, "We are the best in this critical area." Everyone in your organization should know exactly where and why your company and your products or services are *superior* to every other competitor in the market. If you are not better than your competitors somewhere, somehow, in a market-specific area, then all you can hope for is survival, and the only way you can sell is by lowering your prices.

If you don't have a clear competitive advantage, you have to ask: "What *should* my competitive advantage be if I want to survive and thrive in this market?" What *could* it be? How could you make your offering stand out from your competitor's products in a way that your customers will say, "That is a better product or service for me than what else is being offered."

Discovering, developing, and promoting your "uniqueness" is the vital factor in market leadership and superior profitability. It should be made clear in all of your promotional materials. Thinking about competitive advantage all day and all night is a key focus for any successful business.

The Marketing Mix

The marketing mix is often described using the seven "Ps." A change in any one of these key factors can change your business and your results immediately.

1. **Product (or Service):** What exactly does your product or service do for your customers? How could it be changed or improved? What other products could you offer? What products or services should you *stop* selling because of changing market conditions and customer tastes?

2. **Price:** How much do you charge, and how do you charge it? Do you, or should you, charge more or less, or should you charge differently, for the product or service to increase your sales?

3. **Promotion:** This combination of marketing—how you *attract* new customers and sales—determines how you *convert* interested prospects into buying customers. Any change in your marketing and sales activities can change your business.

4. **Place:** Where is your product sold, delivered, serviced? Of the countless different ways and places to sell a product, most companies only use one or two. Where else could you offer and sell your product or service?

5. **Packaging:** This *visual* component of your products, services, company facilities, and every factor that the customers see may influence their buying decisions. How can you differentiate your products and services with packaging to make them more desirable?

6. **Positioning:** The way you are thought about and *described* in the market by your customers and competitors—especially

the *words* that are used to refer to your products, services and management—is the essence of this factor.

7. **People:** This factor is perhaps the most important of all. These people interact with your customers and can be either a positive or negative influence on customers' decisions. Who are the key people inside and outside your business who determine your level of sales?

Successful marketing requires that you continually evaluate the elements of the marketing mix. If your products or services are not selling up to your expectations, usually one or more factors in the marketing mix require alteration. This mix needs to be continually reviewed, rethought, and revised in order to yield higher sales and greater profitability.

Customer-Focused Marketing

Successful marketing places the customer at the center of all planning and decision making. Everybody in the company is focused on the customer at all times. Employees need to develop an obsession with customer service. They communicate with, interact with, and stay close to their customers. Continual personal contact and market research are essential to ongoing customer satisfaction.

In Buck Rogers's book on IBM, he says that every single person in the corporation looks at themselves as a customer service representative. Your company will be successful to the degree to which every single person—including the people who sweep the floor, drive the truck, or answer the telephone—in *your* company thinks about the customers all the time.

A metaphysical law of concentration states that "whatever you dwell upon grows." Whatever you think about continually, and reflect upon intensely, grows in your reality. If you make your customers the central focus of your attention, you will find better, cheaper, easier, and faster ways to satisfy them, and they will reward you by coming back over and over again.

Positioning Strategies

One of the most important parts of marketing for major market penetration is your positioning strategy, or structuring yourself in the market One of the richest men in the world, Sam Walton of Walmart, started off with a discount clothing store in Bentonville, Arkansas. He had one simple concept: He wanted to be perceived as a store that cared about its customers and supplied good-quality merchandise at fair prices. Not the lowest prices, but good quality at fair prices. He managed to achieve that perception to the point of making Walmart the most successful retailing operation in history.

Ask yourself what perception you want to create? How would it be *useful* for you to be viewed by your customer: Quality leader? Service leader? Low price leader? What could you do, starting today, to begin creating that perception?

The perception that you generate on the outside can only be accomplished if you make fundamental critical changes on the inside. In other words, you cannot create a false perception that is lasting. A perception must be a real reflection of the internal structure and values of the organization.

Creative Marketing: Four Growth Strategies

The more you think about these strategies, the more ideas you will generate. The four basic creative marketing strategies are:

1. You can sell more of your current products in your existing markets by modifying them, advertising more effectively, bundling them, expanding your distribution, or lowering your price.

2. You can sell new products and services in your existing markets to your existing customers. What other offerings could you create to complement your current products and services, in places you have already established credibility and distribution channels?

3. You can sell your existing products into *new* markets. How can you continually seek out new markets to target with your products and services, both nationally and internationally?

4. You can create new products to sell in completely new markets. What new products and services could you develop for new markets using your existing capabilities, resources, people, and production facilities?

Bundle of Resources Concept

One of the most important marketing concepts is called "the bundle of resources" concept. As a mental exercise, look at your company as a bundle of resources capable of many things. Focus primarily on your human, intellectual, and production resources. This assessment can help free you from the limitation of thinking only in terms of the products and services you have now, with the customers and markets you are now serving. Think of your company as being capable of producing a variety of profitable products or services for your existing or new markets.

It may be a good idea to establish a new business or division to explore new possibilities to sell new products and services to new markets with new distribution channels. In any case, fully 80 percent of your products and services will be obsolete within five years, and maybe much sooner. To survive and grow, you will have to be offering something new and different. You should be thinking today about what those new products and services might be.

Market Testing for Fast Feedback

Market research is critical to your success. One basic rule for product marketing states, "Test, test, test." No matter how much you test, you are still not guaranteed success. But if you don't do market testing, you're almost certain to fail.

Go directly to a potential customer and describe the product or service you're considering, including the price and the product's benefits. Ask for the customer's opinion of it. Most customers will tell you right away whether it sounds like a good idea. Then, produce a basic model or prototype as fast as you possibly can and test it in the market. Always assume that a competitor is rushing to bring a similar product or service to the market, and you want to be first.

The only real test of a product is a market test. Only by taking it into the marketplace and offering it to customers can you really tell whether a product or service is going to be successful. The sooner you get a market test, the more accurate and successful you will be.

In this process, you need to aim for immediate feedback. When we were developing seminars some years ago, we had a simple strategy. We would design a seminar we thought people would want, need, and be willing to pay for. Then we would send out 5,000 pieces of mail, get on a couple of interview shows, and advertise in the newspaper to see how many people actually came out to attend the seminar. We could tell within 30 days whether we had a winner. This approach made it possible for us to develop a series of successful seminars.

In the final analysis, all marketing is aimed at increasing profitability by doing the right things right. If you practice these key principles of market strategy, nothing can stop you from being an excellent marketer and achieving ever-higher levels of sales and profitability.

Action Exercises

1. Determine your area of competitive advantage, what your product or service offers that makes it superior to any other product or service in your market.
2. List three ways that you could sell more of your product in your existing markets.
3. Decide upon three ways that you could test the potential of your new product idea before you invest time and money in creating and marketing it.
4. Identify your main competitors, those companies or influences that determine how much you sell and at what price.

5. List the additional products you could develop and bring to the market with your existing resources.

6. List three elements of the marketing mix that you could change in some way to increase your sales in the months ahead.

7. What could you do immediately to offset the perceptions customers have of your competitors' advantages? How could you make your products more attractive than those of your competitors?

CHAPTER SEVEN

THE DISCIPLINE
OF CREATIVITY

*"You have more potential than you could use in one
hundred lifetimes; there is no problem you cannot
solve, no goal you cannot achieve, by unlocking the
power of your mind."*

—Brian Tracy

Creative thinking skills are vital to your success. The average manager
spends 50 percent or more of his time solving problems, either alone
or with others. Your ability to deal with difficulties and solve problems will, more than anything else, determine everything that happens
in your career. In fact, it is safe to say that an individual with poor creative thinking skills will be always relegated to working for those with
developed creative thinking skills.

Creativity is a skill, like riding a bicycle or operating a computer, that can be learned and developed with practice. Creativity is
a discipline that you can develop with practice and repetition, until
it becomes a natural extension of your personality and your skill set.
Often a direct relationship becomes apparent between the *quantity*
of new ideas that you generate in your work and the level of success
you achieve. One new idea or insight can be enough to change the
direction of an entire company. The profitability, income, and
future prospects for you and your company depend on your creative
contribution.

Remember, everything that you are or ever will be comes as the result of the way you use your mind. If you improve the quality of your thinking, you improve the quality of your life.

Let's begin with a whole new way of looking at the world.

Defining Creativity

The best single definition of creativity is "improvement." Every single idea that improves the way we live and work, in large or small ways, is an act of creativity. The more you look for ways to improve activities and circumstances on a day-to-day basis, the more creative you become. Your creativity is a latent force deep down in your intelligence. You can become more creative by placing more demands on your creative capability.

Every single person has what is called a "line of sight." In each organization the line of sight is what you see when you look up; it's the job you do and everything that is going on around you. And everyone can find ways to improve what is going on in their line of sight. Success in business life is directly proportionate to the quantity of new ideas that you come up with on a day-to-day and week-to-week basis. Someone who comes up with a continuous stream of good ideas, or even average ideas, is destined for great success in business. People who come up with few or no ideas are usually stuck where they are. Look in your line of sight. How can you improve the way you are doing your work? How can you increase your results or lower your costs?

Ask for Suggestions

In 1975, Mazda Corporation of Japan had been decimated as a result of trying to introduce and perfect the rotary engine. Its profits were down to $5 million. In desperation, it introduced a program that encouraged people in the company to give suggestions on how Mazda could do things better, faster, easier, or cheaper. They were astonished at the results! In the first year, they received more than 200,000 suggestions and implemented 60 percent, or 120,000, of them. Mazda made another interesting discovery. Although it had an excellent reward system for good suggestions, the greatest satisfaction the employees received came from coming up with an idea and seeing it applied.

Five years later, in 1980, Mazda Corporation had made an astonishing turnaround; its profits were up to $95 million, the suggestions were running at 2 million per year at an astonishing 60 percent implementation. Profits had increased 1,800 percent. Officials at Mazda said that the reason for these results was the suggestion system that encouraged each person to contribute his or her creativity to the well-being of the company.

When researchers measured the level of implementation of suggestions in North American corporations, it ran about 10 percent, which means that for every 10 suggestions collected, nine were *rejected*. What does it do to a workforce to have 90 percent of its creative input rejected? Employees eventually conclude, "What the heck! Forget it. It's not worth it." Even worse than that, many companies encourage suggestions and then simply ignore them if they are inconvenient or if they cost any time or money to try out. What these companies are missing is an awareness of the apparent direct relationship between ideas and profitability. The greater the number of ideas submitted, the greater will be the quality of the ideas implemented. Small incremental improvements to cut costs, increase quality, and boost customer or employee satisfaction can translate into huge increases in profitability.

Because of the dynamic and competitive nature of our society and the acceleration of obsolescence, the more and better ideas you can generate in your organization, the more likely it is that you will survive and thrive in the years ahead. An organization that does not continually come up with new ideas is doomed.

The Root Source of Creativity

Creativity is a natural, spontaneous characteristic of *positive* individuals with high self-esteem. Companies that create positive corporate environments receive a steady flow of ideas from everyone on staff.

Three factors influence the number of creative ideas a person generates. The first is past experiences, which have a lot to do with how creative you are. If you've been in environments in the past where ideas have been encouraged, you'll probably have a positive attitude and aptitude for coming up with new ideas. If you've been in a negative environment, your creativity will likely be dulled.

The second factor is your current situation. Do you find a lot of encouragement for new ideas in your present circumstances? Do people laugh and get involved, or do they ridicule or criticize?

The third factor is your *self-image*. Do you consider yourself to be a creative person? It is thought that fully 95 percent of people have the ability to come up with good ideas. In fact, the work done by Howard Gardner at Harvard University suggests that each person is a potential *genius* in at least one area. Therefore, the starting point of unlocking your creativity is to for you to begin to think of yourself as a highly creative person.

You Are a Potential Genius

Repeat this statement to yourself over and over again: "I'm a genius!" At first, it may sound and feel a little silly. Initially, your subconscious mind may resist the idea. But your subconscious mind has stored away every single bit of information and experience you have ever had in your life, like a massive data base it can draw upon. After continually repeating "I'm a genius," over and over, your subconscious will eventually begin to reassemble data in the form of ideas to help you solve the problems you're wrestling with today. Even if it feels funny at the start, just keep repeating, "I'm a genius, I'm a genius!"

I've had hundreds of graduates of my seminars come back to me and say they were amazed how smart they became when they began to deliberately change their self-images and affirm repeatedly that they were creative and innovative.

Move Out of Your Comfort Zone

A major barrier to creativity is "the comfort zone." People have a natural tendency to resist new ideas, to say *no* to anything new or different. Does your company encourage people to take risks and to suggest new ways of doing things? Do you as a manager?

A direct relationship in an organization connects happiness, on the one hand, and optimism and creativity on the other. Happy, valued employees and executives are always more creative. Whenever people feel valued, important, and respected in an organization, creativity bubbles forth naturally. Optimism, cheerfulness, positive expectancy, and laughter all trigger creativity. What do you do to reward, recognize, and reinforce your staff when they come up with new ideas?

The fact is that everybody is inherently creative. It is a gift provided to you by nature to deal with the problems and challenges of life. The only difference is that some people use a lot of their creativity, and some use very little. On average, a person driving to and from work probably has about *four ideas* per year, any one of which could make him or her a millionaire if he or she were to pursue it. The reason we don't pursue our ideas is because we don't believe that they could be of any value. The fact is that you may have *forty ideas* every year, any one of which would enable you to fulfill all your dreams.

The quality of calm confidence in your creativity is one of the most powerful forces you can develop to stimulate your subconscious mind into giving you good ideas. Your job is to accept that you really are a genius and that ideas come to you naturally and in abundance.

Three Triggers to Creativity

Normal creativity is stimulated by three factors:

1. **Intensely desired goals.** Intense emotion of any kind is a stimulant or trigger to creativity. The more you want something, the more likely it is you will find creative ways to accomplish it. That's why it is said that there are no uncreative people, just those without goals that they want badly enough. What are your most intensely desired goals?

2. **Pressing problems.** If a problem or an obstacle is stopping you from achieving something that is important to you, you'll be amazed at how creative you become in your ability to remove it.

3. **Focused questions**. The more precise and focused the questions you ask yourself and others, the more rapidly the creative reflex operates to generate workable answers.

Testing your assumptions can be a more specific way of asking focused questions and getting at the heart of your goals and the obstacles to them. Continually ask yourself, "What are my assumptions?" Question not only your obvious ones, but also what may be your *hidden* assumptions. Most importantly, really look at where your assumptions might be wrong. False assumptions lie at the root of every failure. Whenever you are facing real trouble or difficulty, ask yourself, "What are my assumptions in this situation?"

Problem Solving Made Simple

Any organized method of problem solving is more effective in generating higher-quality solutions than no method at all. Here are six steps you can follow:

1. Define the problem clearly—in writing. Accurate diagnosis is half the cure. What exactly is the problem? Fuzzy definitions are major obstacles to problem solving.
2. Read, research, and gather information. Get the facts. Many problems exist because no one has gathered sufficient information. Often, with enough information, the solution becomes obvious.
3. Ask questions of informed people and consult experts. Go to the Internet. Do a search with Google's Keywords. Almost every problem you will ever have has already been solved by someone.
4. Try *consciously* to solve the problem. Think of everything you can possibly do, and then, if you don't get an answer, simply let it go. Release the problem completely and get your mind busy elsewhere. Turn the problem over to your subconscious mind; it will work on it 24 hours per day.
5. Review the problem just before sleeping, and ask your subconscious for a solution. Take a few minutes before you go to sleep

to write out your next day's schedule and think about the problems or difficulties you may have to face, and then turn them over to your subconscious mind. You may wake up in the middle of the night with the answer, the "eureka factor."

6. Write it down. If you don't write down your ideas when they come to you, or dictate them quickly into your smartphone or recorder, you can easily forget them.

Sometimes one good idea can save you years of hard work. One good idea can be all you need to start a fortune. Capture it on paper.

The Mindstorming Method

Mindstorming is one of the most powerful ways ever discovered to solve problems and achieve goals. It provides a way of using focused questions for concentrating the power of your mind. More people have become wealthy using this simple method than any other type of creative thinking or problem-solving technique. It is often called "the 20 idea method."

Take a clean sheet of paper. Write your most pressing problem or goal at the top of the page in the form of a question. For example, if your goal is to increase your sales from $250,000 to $350,000 in the next 12 months, you would write "What can we do to increase our sales to $350,000 in the next 12 months?" The more specific the question, the better quality of answers you will stimulate.

You then begin writing answers to the question. You discipline yourself to keep writing until you get to 20 answers, or more. You can do this on your own or with a group of people using a whiteboard or flipchart.

When you first use this method, the first five answers will be fairly easy. The next five answers will be more difficult, and the last ten answers will be *really* difficult. But over and over, we have found that often the twentieth answer is the breakthrough idea that changes everything.

Generating Ideas

Write down the first idea you think of, and then write down the *opposite* of it. Then write down a synthesis of the two. Write down even ridiculous answers. Just force yourself to write a minimum of 20 answers, and surprisingly enough, sometimes an answer will leap off the page at you. One of my students found that his seventeenth answer was the solution he had been seeking for more than six months. When he implemented it, it changed his business completely.

Once you have generated at least 20 ideas, select at one (or more) idea from your list and implement it immediately. This action keeps your creative juices flowing. If you use this technique first thing in the morning, you will more likely be functioning at a higher level of creativity and intelligence all day long. And the more you practice this method, the more creative and alert you will become.

Questioning to Stimulate Creativity

Your creative mind is stimulated and triggered into action by *focused questions*. The more questions you ask, and the more provocative they are, the more accurate and creative will be your thinking. Focused questions are the mark of a truly intelligent person. If you learn to ask focused questions of yourself, you can then ask focused questions of other people.

Some of the best questions you can ask in business are:

- What are we trying to do?
- How are we trying to do it?
- What result or outcome are we trying to achieve?
- What would be our perfect result or solution?
- What are our assumptions?
- Could these assumptions be wrong? (Remember that errant assumptions lie at the root of every failure.)
- What do we do now?

Developing the Qualities of Genius

Genius is not a matter of IQ. It is more a way of acting and thinking than of inborn intelligence. Studies of geniuses throughout the ages indicate that they all have *three* habits of mind in common.

First, geniuses have the ability to concentrate single-mindedly, 100 percent, on one subject, to the exclusion of all else. Today, the greatest enemy of creative thinking is *distraction*, of all kinds. Because you are surrounded by so many technological devices, it is increasing difficult to focus, but focus you must if you want to tap into your amazing creative powers.

Try this: Write down every detail of the problem you are working on right now. "Swarm all over it." Sometimes the very act of writing out all the details stimulates ideas and solutions.

A second characteristic of geniuses is their ability to see *causal* relationships among various factors. They can see the big picture. Geniuses retain an open-minded, flexible, and almost childlike attitude toward examining every possible way of approaching a problem, without rushing to a conclusion.

Try looking at your work, yourself, and your business as part of an organic system. This approach means considering how each factor affects and influences other factors. Instead of looking at the event as a discrete and separate experience, look at all the things that might have led up to the event and all the things that might occur after the event. Think of your situation as part of a bigger picture and consider all the different interrelationships.

Avoid the tendency to develop an *attachment* to a solution or idea. One of the factors that puts the brakes on creative thinking is becoming attached or falling in love with an idea we've come up with. Then we invest our ego in selling the idea to others. Instead, resolve to stay detached from the idea initially, and consider as many *other* ideas as possible with an open mind. Stay flexible, even with an idea that seems fantastic. Avoid the natural tendency to embrace your idea until you've looked at all possibilities.

Third, geniuses use a systematic, orderly approach to solving each problem, as they teach in mathematics or physics. All geniuses approach problems systematically rather than in a random or haphazard way. They ask questions such as: Why? Why not? Why not this way? Could there be another way? They have the ability to suspend judgment and to avoid becoming attached to, or enamored of, their own ideas until they have explored them completely.

Mind-Stimulating Exercises

Here are some key questions to stimulate your creativity. Take a few minutes to write your own answers to each question before moving on.

1. What are your three most important goals in life right now?
2. What are your three most pressing problems right now?
3. Describe the ideal outcome you desire from a problem facing you right now.
4. What one thing would you dare to attempt if you knew you could not fail?
5. And my favorite, "What do you really want to do with your life?"

These questions stimulate your creativity and open your mind to greater possibilities.

Identifying Key Obstacles

On the path to achieving any goal there will be obstacles; some of which you can see and others you cannot. Your creativity should be focused on removing the biggest obstacle to your success at the moment. This obstacle is a "rock" on your road to success and happiness. You must somehow get around, over, or through this major rock in order to achieve your most important goal.

Identifying your major rock and focusing all your creative energies on moving that obstacle out of your path will help you make more progress than if you were to remove all the other smaller obstacles in your way. The biggest mistake that people make is to do what is fun and easy rather than what is right, necessary, and difficult. They focus on the little obstacles and small day-to-day problems. They ignore the massive rock that is the primary obstacle holding them back. This obstacle is often called the "limiting factor."

In every process, the limiting factor is what determines the speed at which the goal will be accomplished. You have to ask, in your work and business, what is the limiting factor? It may be education or knowledge. It may be money. It may be a key skill or ability. What is the one thing standing in the way of you achieving the successes you desire? Once you've identified it, swarm all over it. Devote your energies to getting rid of the major obstacle, before you do anything else.

Brainstorming

Brainstorming is a powerful technique for developing synergy in an organization. A chief responsibility for effective managers is to conduct regular brainstorming sessions focused on business improvements.

The process of brainstorming is simple:

- The ideal number for a brainstorming session is four to seven people.
- The length of the session should be 15 to 45 minutes long. Thirty minutes is optimal.
- Define the question or problem clearly so that everyone knows and agrees.
- Write down the idea so everyone can see it during the session.
- Strive for the greatest number of ideas, without evaluation. Don't stop to judge or question them, just try for as many ideas or solutions as you can generate in the time allocated.
- Accept every idea without comment, except to say something like, "That's a good idea!" to encourage more ideas. The more people laugh in a brainstorming session the more likely you are to come up with great ideas.

- Appoint a recorder who writes down every idea no matter how wild the idea may sound, for evaluation later.
- The leader acts only as the facilitator and does not dominate the conversation. The facilitator encourages everybody to contribute. If you're the manager and leader, the less you say the better.
- If you're also the recorder, just add your ideas silently to the list.

At the end of the brainstorming session, gather up all the ideas for evaluation at a later time, preferably by someone who is not a participant in the session. This step helps to keep ego out of the process.

Nominal Group Technique

This technique is used in brainstorming or mindstorming to elicit creative answers to specific problems. The simplest example is sentence-completion exercises. Complete the following three sentences with as many different answers as possible.

1. We could double our sales if . . .
2. We could cut our costs by 20 percent if . . .
3. We could defeat our competition in the marketplace if . . .

Regular practice of this method will greatly increase the quality and quantity of creative thinking of everyone. This process is a good way to find solutions that are right under your nose, but you might not have recognized them yet.

Lateral Thinking Methods

Lateral thinking forces the mind out of comfortable or conventional ways of thinking. It was pioneered by Edward De Bono. The best way to describe this process is that when people find themselves in a hole, the natural tendency is to dig the hole deeper, when actually the correct solution may be to dig a totally different hole. Lateral thinking is a way of breaking yourself of the tendency to keep doing things the same old way.

You can *reverse* key words or phrases. For example, you can call a problem an opportunity. With that in mind you look into it and seek the opportunity it may contain. Instead of saying, "Sales are down," say, "purchases are down." It's not that we are not selling enough, but our customers are not buying enough. This twist changes the whole focus of the discussion.

Random association requires that you select words and force them to fit a particular situation. Take a word such as *orange* or *artichoke* and describe your business, product, or problem as that word. "Our business is like an orange because. . . ." On the outside, it looks quite smooth, but as you get closer, you see a lot of bumps. Inside you find a lot of seeds and separations. There are also some juicy parts. In what way does your business look like an orange, inside and out?

Identify *the dominant idea*. If the dominant idea is that "we have a real problem here," maybe the dominant idea should be that "we have a real profit opportunity." Shift your thinking away from the dominant idea. For example, rather than saying, "We need to sell more," say, "Our customers need to buy more." Maybe a loss that you're suffering will enable you to make a profit by doing or changing to something else.

Look at *the other person's viewpoint* and try to see and describe the situation through that person's eyes. Lawyers use this approach when preparing a case for court. They will think about arguing the case from the opponent's point of view before preparing their own case.

Finally, *fantasize*. It is a wonderful way of thinking creatively. Imagine that you had a magic wand you could wave to remove all obstacles to achieving your objectives. If that were to happen—you waved it and all your problems disappeared—what would your situation look like?

Value-Engineering Principle

Value engineering is a simple method of evaluating the usefulness of a new product by asking some key questions.

1. What is it? Describe it through the mind of the consumer.
2. What does it do?
3. What does it cost?
4. What else will do the same job?
5. What does that cost?

Often such an examination will lead you to outsourcing. You may find that instead of doing something in-house, you could find another company that has better capacities or facilities and save money by having them do the job.

Evaluating Your Ideas

Ideas are a dime a dozen. Eighty percent of new products introduced after research and testing fail, and 99 percent of ideas are impractical. Before falling in love with your ideas, subject them to rigorous evaluation. First of all, is it effective? Will it work? Will it make a meaningful difference? Is it a good enough idea to make a meaningful improvement? Is it compatible with human nature? Is it compatible with the way people like to shop?

Today, people will shop online for the things they want, and then get in their car to pick them up at the retailer. Why? Because people like to touch, handle, taste, smell, and feel things. They like the experience of live shopping. Conversely, today people visit retailers to see the product personally and then go home and buy it online. This approach is called "showrooming." How will these behaviors affect the shopping patterns of customers in the future? How will it affect your customers?

When you think about your idea, is it compatible with your goals? Is it an idea to which you or someone else can make a total commitment? If it is not compatible with what you want to accomplish in your life so that you can commit yourself wholeheartedly, maybe you should pass it on to someone else.

Is the timing right? Is it practical now? Sometimes an idea is too soon or too late. A great idea for a luxury product is likely to have trouble catching on in the middle of a recession. Similarly, a discount item may flop in a boom time.

Is it feasible? Is it worth it to engage in the activity and cost to produce and deliver it? What other opportunities are available that will require the same amount of time and money to develop and test?

Finally, is it simple? In the final analysis almost all great innovations are simple. They can be explained in 25 words or less. The customer in the marketplace can hear a description of the innovation and say "Yes, that's good. That's what I want. I'll take it. That's what I need."

Simplicity is the key because it has to be sold by ordinary people, and ordinary people are not necessarily competent. It has to be bought by ordinary people, and ordinary people are not geniuses; they may not easily comprehend the product or its true value if it cannot be explained simply.

Each person becomes a genius to the degree to which he exercises his creative faculties. Regularly applying the questions and exercises in this chapter to your personal and business activities, you will develop within yourself the discipline of creativity, which you can then use for the rest of your career.

Action Exercises

1. Write down your three most important business goals right now.
2. Write down your three biggest business problems, challenges, or obstacles to greater sales and profitability right now.
3. Practice mindstorming on one of your problems by defining it as question and then generating 20 answers to that question.
4. Assemble a group of four to seven people in your business to brainstorm on one of your problems or goals for 15–45 minutes.
5. Complete the sentence, "We could double our sales (or profitability) over the next 12 months if we . . ." with as many answers as possible.

6. Identify your limiting factor to greater business success. What one factor sets the speed at which you achieve your most important business goal, and how could you remove it?
7. Identify your assumptions about yourself, your business, and your products, services, and markets, and then ask, "What if these assumptions were not true?" What would you do then?

CHAPTER EIGHT

THE DISCIPLINE OF COURAGE

"Courage is the ladder on which all the other virtues mount."

—Clare Boothe Luce

Leaders throughout the ages have been studied in an attempt to determine the qualities that make them exceptional in their time and situation. More than 50 leadership qualities have been identified. But of all of these qualities, the two that all leaders seem to have in common are vision and courage.

Leaders formulate a clear vision of where they want to take their organization in the long term. Being able to articulate this vision clearly is the key to motivating and inspiring others to work with them to make that vision a reality.

The second leadership quality that all the studies found in common was *courage*. Leaders have the courage to do whatever is necessary to achieve their vision. The development of courage in a leader is essential to realizing his or her full potential. Fortunately, courage can be learned and developed over time by engaging in certain behaviors over and over again.

Courage Is the Golden Mean

Aristotle is famous for his concept of the "golden mean" of virtues, as he described in his "Nicomachean Ethics." He described courage as the golden mean between the extremes of impetuosity on the one end, and cowardice at the other end. He taught that the way to move from one extreme to the other was to overcompensate in the opposite direction from where you are today. For example, then, if you felt afraid or cowardly, you would force yourself to act impetuously; boldly going to that extreme until you eventually came back and settled down at the golden mean of courage.

Aristotle also said that the way to develop any virtue is to act as if you *already* had that virtue in every situation where that virtue is required. Psychologists call this the "law of reversibility." It says that if you act in a particular way, you will eventually trigger the thoughts and feelings that would accompany those actions. By continually acting as if you already had the qualities you desire, you eventually develop those qualities as a part of your character where they become a permanent part of your personality.

Everyone Is Afraid

The fact is that everyone is afraid; the only difference is in the things we are afraid of and with what degree of intensity. For you to be a great leader, you must develop the quality of courage and use it to deal with the trials, tribulations, and turbulence of leadership, especially in today's business environment.

The two greatest fears we all share are the fears of failure and loss on the one hand, and the fears of criticism and rejection on the other. Many other fears include poverty, embarrassment, ridicule, loss of love, loss of security or status, and so on. But all of these fears fall under one of the two umbrella categories mentioned: failure and rejection.

What is the difference, then, between the brave person and the coward? Both are afraid, but the brave person forces himself or herself to act in spite of a fear. Emerson wrote, "Do the thing you fear, and the death of fear is certain." The only way to free yourself from fear is to do what you fear. It is for you to move *toward* the fear-inducing circumstance or person and as you do, the fear actually becomes smaller and more manageable. But if you back away from the fear, if you avoid the fear-causing situation or person, the fear grows larger and larger and soon dominates your thoughts and feelings.

Identify Your Biggest Goal

One of the questions we often ask in our seminars is, "What one great goal would you dare to set for yourself if you knew you could not fail?" If you were absolutely guaranteed success in any one thing in life, big or small, short or long term, what one great goal would you set for yourself?

Another question we ask is, "What have you always wanted to do but been afraid to attempt?" Often, your answer to this question indicates what you are really meant to do with your life. The things that you have been afraid to attempt in the past may be in the area where you could enjoy the greatest success and happiness, if you could just overcome your fears in that area. Your answers to each of these questions will often reveal the role that fear plays in your current decisions.

The biggest fears that most people have today break down into financial fears on the one hand, and fears of confrontation or dealing with difficult people on the other. Many companies get into serious difficulties because of the top executive's fear of dealing with a negative or underperforming person in a key job.

You can reduce your financial fears with better planning, by organizing your financial life to live debt free and with sufficient cash reserves so that you don't have to worry about money. You can resolve your people fears by confronting the difficult people in your life and putting an end to the negative situation that is making you unhappy. When you confront your fears, and do the thing you fear, your self-confidence and self-esteem immediately improve. But when you avoid your fears, wishing and hoping they would go away, your neocortex (the reasoning and thinking center of your brain) shuts down and you withdraw to your animal brain, or limbic system, which has only two settings—fight or flight. When pulled between the fight or flight reactions, you will be either angry or depressed. Neither of these conditions is conducive to good decision making.

Where Courage Is Required

Courage is required, and even demanded, in several areas of business life. The first area is in *decision making*. It takes courage to make important decisions that involve the irrevocable commitment of money and resources, especially when the outcome cannot be guaranteed.

Leaders do not like to fail. They do everything possible to avoid failure by minimizing risk. But they know that failure is inevitable and unavoidable in the pursuit of sales and profits. It is impossible to succeed without failing, sometimes over and over again, until you learn the vital lessons necessary to succeed at a high level. The key is to "fail forward," which means using trial and error to enable you as a leader and your organization to learn and move forward. As Herodotus said, "There is no shame in failing; only in not rising again."

Types of Decisions

Decision making is a key skill and responsibility of leadership. It is important to recognize what type of decision you need to make:

1. *Decisions that you have to make:* These issues are your chief responsibility. No one else can make these decisions. If you don't make them, others cannot act. The system slows down and then stops.
2. *Decisions that you don't have to make:* Sometimes you can simply remain neutral, or buy time, rather than making a decision you cannot then get out of.
3. *Decisions that are not yours to make:* These decisions are the responsibility of someone else, who then becomes responsible for carrying out the decision. One of the best ways to build competence and confidence in people is to delegate decision making to them, and then work with them to learn and grow through the process.

4. *Decisions that you cannot **not** make:* In the absence of a decision in this area, nothing gets done. Progress stops, and no advancement is possible.

If you are experiencing fear about making decisions, it is important to recognize that one of the main causes of fear is ignorance. It is fear of the unknown. You can greatly reduce this fear, and this block to decision making, by doing more research, by gathering more information.

Risk Taking

Another area where courage is required is in the area of *risk taking*. The fact is that every action or decision entails risk. We never have any guarantee that an action or decision will be successful.

Many people believe that entrepreneurs and business people are "risk takers." Sometimes politicians encourage businesses to "take more risks," to hire more people and stimulate the economy. But the fact is that *successful* business people and entrepreneurs are really "risk avoiders." They do everything possible to minimize the risks involved in the pursuit of sales and profitability. They engage in due diligence and conduct careful research. They get as much information as possible to reduce the possibility of loss, both of time and money.

As a leader, you face several types of risk:

1. *The risks you have to take:* No progress is possible without moving forward into the unknown.
2. *The risks that are not yours to take:* They are the responsibility of someone else, like hiring a new person.
3. *The risks that you can afford to take:* The upside can be especially positive, the costs are low, and the downside is small.
4. *The risks you cannot **not** take:* These risks involve possible loss, but the upside for you and your company are so great if you succeed that you must take this type of risk.

Analyze each risk and determine into which category it falls. This process of assessing the actual risk reduces your fears and increases your courage.

Two Parts of Courage

The first part of courage is the courage to *begin*—to launch, to step out in faith, to "go boldly where no man has gone before." The second part of courage is the courage to *endure*—to continue, to persist in the face of the inevitable short-term failure and temporary setbacks. This part of courage is called "courageous patience"; it is the ability to hang in there, to be resolute and determined, particularly in the period between when you launch a new product or endeavor and when you experience any results or success.

"Stay the course!" has always been an excellent piece of advice. Often it is too early to tell whether your decision is going to succeed. It is amazing how many people lose heart and pull the plug on an initiative just before it succeeds. As Ross Perot said, "Many people quit just before succeeding. That's not the time to quite, but the time to exert even greater effort."

The development of courage is essential to your success as a leader. You can eventually become fearless and unstoppable by practicing some of these ideas until they become entrenched habits and disciplines of both mind and action.

Action Exercises

1. Identify one area or situation in your life where fear may be holding you back, and resolve today to confront the fear situation or the person directly and deal with it once and for all.
2. Think of the biggest risk you are taking in your life today and determine whether it is your risk to take, or if it is too big a risk to take.
3. Identify the most important decisions you will have to make in the future, and determine what you would decide if you had no fear of failure.

4. In what areas of your life and work could the fear of rejection or the fear of criticism or disapproval of others be holding you back from taking action?
5. In what area do you need to act boldly, to launch into a new endeavor, even if you have no guarantees of success?
6. In what areas do you need to endure, to persist, to keep on working, even if you feel discouraged?
7. Identify the three most important lessons that you have learned from failure in the past, and how they have helped you to be a better person today.

CHAPTER NINE

THE DISCIPLINE OF CARING ABOUT PEOPLE

"It doesn't matter how much you know; all that really matters is how much you care.
—Anonymous

How much do you really care about the people who work for you? This question is central to determining your success as a leader and the success of your organization.

Here is a question for you: How much of people's thinking and decision making is emotional, and how much is logical? The answer is that people are 100 percent emotional. They decide emotionally and then justify logically. To put it another way, the way your people *feel* about you, the company, your products and services, and themselves when they are at work, is the critical element in their performance, productivity, and output. The way they feel determines their levels of engagement and how involved, dedicated, committed, and creative they are. And this emotional factor is largely influenced by the manager and the way he or she treats people on a daily basis.

Your Greatest Resource

The greatest untapped resource in any organization, and the most expensive, is its people. It is within the skills and abilities of the average person where the greatest potential for growth, productivity, performance, achievement, and profitability lies.

In this chapter, you will learn one of the most important disciplines of management—to focus on the emotional component of your work and how to motivate others to peak performance. You will learn how to use some of the best ideas developed in the past 50 years to enable your people to feel terrific about themselves and to contribute their maximum to the organization.

All motivation is self-motivation. You cannot motivate people from the outside, but you can remove the obstacles that stop them from motivating themselves. As a manager, you can create an environment where this potential and motivation is released naturally and spontaneously.

Tap Into Your Human Resources

According to Robert Half and Associates, the average person works at about 50 percent of capability. The other 50 percent is largely wasted throughout the working day in idle conversation with coworkers, playing on the Internet, coming in late, leaving early, extended coffee breaks and lunches, and personal business.

One of the reasons for this time wastage, one of the greatest financial drains on any organization, is that people are not motivated and focused enough on their work and lack the urgency and direction to get their work done before they do anything else. They often do not feel that their boss or the company really cares about them as individuals. It is, however, a challenge that a good manager can resolve. Your job then is to tap into the unused 50 percent that the company is paying for and to channel that time and energy into producing more and better work.

The purpose of a business is to get the highest ROE (return on equity) from the amount of capital invested in the company. The goal of management is to get the highest ROE (return on energy) from the people who work there. Financial capital is calculated in dollars. Human capital consists of the mental, emotional, and physical energies of the individual. Your job as a manager is to maximize this human capital and focus it on achieving the most valuable and important results possible for the organization.

Remove the De-Motivators

The two major de-motivators in life and work are both factors that begin in early childhood and carry forward into adult life. They are often referred to as negative habit patterns or conditioned responses to stimuli.

Removing Fear of Failure

The first of these de-motivators is the *fear of failure*. It is the greatest single obstacle to success and achievement in adult life. Because of destructive criticism in childhood, the adult grows up afraid of making a mistake or failing at his or her work. This fear serves as a form of paralysis and holds people back from taking risks, volunteering for new responsibilities, or extending themselves in any way. Fear of failure holds people back from taking on new assignments and continually create reasons or excuses for nonperformance.

In the research on *A Great Place to Work*, which is updated each year, one of the key factors identified in high-performance organizations is simply called "trust." They define trust as "the ability to make a mistake at work without being criticized or punished."

Making People Feel Safe

A quality of high-performance organizations is that the people in them are willing to take risks and chances in order to move ahead and to move the company ahead. They are concerned about failing, but not afraid. They know that they can make mistakes and learn from them without the fear of losing their jobs.

W. Edwards Deming, the father of *Total Quality Management*, said that one of the 14 keys to building a high-performance organization was to "drive out fear." In the absence of fear, people tend to perform and produce at a higher level than ever before.

Removing Fear of Rejection

The second major de-motivator is the fear of rejection. This fear arises in early childhood when parents practice "conditional love" on their children. They make their love and support conditional upon the child performing to some undetermined high standard. The child then grows up *hypersensitive* to the opinions, comments, and feedback of others, especially his or her boss in the workplace.

This fear of rejection is also a fear of criticism, condemnation, or censure; the fear of making a mistake and being dumped on for it. Excellent managers are those who practice "unconditional acceptance" with each person, causing them to feel safe and secure with their boss and in their work.

Many other reasons may lead to de-motivation and poor performance, but fears of failure and rejection are the two main fears that prevent individuals from extending themselves to do their best. Successful organizations and managers consciously and deliberately remove these barriers. They encourage creative effort even at the risk of failure or making mistakes. They make it clear that nobody gets rejected, dumped on, criticized, or threatened with retaliation if they make a mistake. The best managers create an environment where people feel free to be the best they can be.

Making People Feel Important

The first part of the word *triumph* is "try." The great discovery is that the more people *like themselves*, value themselves, and consider themselves to be worthwhile human beings, the less they fear failure, the less they fear rejection, and the more willing they are to try new things. They are willing to move out of their "comfort zones" into their "discomfort zones."

Management's job is to encourage "try" in the form of experimentation, greater efforts, and occasional failure in the attempt to find ways to do the work faster, better, and cheaper.

Successful companies create an environment where people feel terrific about themselves. Understanding the role of the self-concept in behavior is the starting point of effectiveness in management and motivation.

The self-concept is the belief structure or value system of the individual. It is a composite of all of the beliefs, values, attitudes, and opinions of the individual, starting in early childhood and continuing to the present day. The self-concept is like the command center that sits at the core of personality and productivity. It is what governs individual performance, behavior, and output.

All changes or improvements in external performance and behavior begin with improvements in the self-concept; the way individuals see and feel about themselves and what they believe about themselves. To put it another way, all changes in the outer world of an individual begin with changes in the inner world.

The Three Parts of Personality

The self-concept is made up of three components: the self-ideal, the self-image, and the self-esteem. Let's take each of these in order.

Support Positive Self-Ideals

The individual's self-ideal is a summary picture of what the person aspires to be in life. It is made up of the goals, dreams, hopes, and ideals the person has and what is possible for him or her to become at some time in the future. Each person is consciously or unconsciously guided and motivated by an inner desire to be more and better at some time in the future.

In the world of work, the individual's self-ideal is influenced by the corporate values, the role models represented by the senior people in the organization, and the corporate culture surrounding employees. When this environment is changed in a positive way, individual employees begin to perform at higher levels.

Build Positive Self-Images

The second part of the self-concept is the *self-image*. It is the way a person thinks he or she is viewed by others. Your self-image is greatly influenced by the way people treat you on a day-to-day basis. When people are treated as though they are valuable, important, and respected, they see themselves and think about themselves in a more positive way. As a result, they perform at higher levels and do better work.

The self-image is also affected by the way the individual sees him- or herself and thinks about him- or herself relative to what he or she is doing. Positive feedback on performance from the boss improves the individual's self-image, and increases his or her ability and desire to perform at a higher level.

Build Self-Esteem in Your People

The third part, and the core of the self-concept, is the individual's level of *self-esteem*. Self-esteem can be defined as "how much you like yourself." The more people like and respect themselves on the inside, the better they perform on the outside. The more people like themselves, the bigger will be the goals that they set for themselves. The more they like themselves, the higher standards they will set for the quality of their work. The more they like themselves, the more they like other people, and the more they become excellent team players. The more they like themselves, the more they perform at higher levels in every area of life.

The key to creating a peak-performing organization is to create a high-self-esteem environment by removing the fears of failure and rejection that inhibit personal performance. The manager who creates a positive, high-self-esteem workplace will have higher performance, lower absenteeism, lower employee turnover, higher productivity, and fewer mistakes.

Focus on the Key Factor

The key factor in motivation and in peak performance is just one thing—the nexus or point of contact between the manager and the managed. It is the key determinant of the performance, productivity, output, and profitability of an organization. The point at which the manager and the managed connect, whether positive or negative, is where the performance of the individual and the organization is determined.

When this contact between the boss and the subordinate is positive, supportive, and encouraging of self-esteem and a positive self-image, then performance, productivity, and output of the individual will be the highest possible. If this point of contact between the manager and the managed is negative for any reason at all, performance and output will decline. A negative relationship with the boss will trigger fears of failure, rejection, and disapproval. If the boss is negative for any reason, people will play it safe and only do exactly what they need to do to avoid being fired.

The more effective you can become in eliciting peak performance from each of your staff members, the more and better people you will be given to manage for peak performance. The top managers and leaders of today are those who are capable of eliciting extraordinary performance from ordinary people.

Effective managers are intensely action-oriented. When they hear a good idea, they move quickly to implement the idea and put it into action. Therefore, if you read about anything you think can help you to motivate your staff to a higher level in this chapter, don't delay. Practice it immediately, that very day. You will be amazed at the results.

Communicate Clear Expectations

Whenever you communicate clear expectations, you make it possible for people to win. Whenever you communicate vague or fuzzy expectations, you risk causing them to fail in doing the right job, or doing it well, and having them end up feeling like losers. The most common complaint in the world of work today is "not knowing what's expected." People need to know exactly what they are expected to do, and when, and to what level of quality.

"You cannot hit a target that you cannot see." In order for your people to feel like winners they need clear goals. The clearer the goals are, the easier it is for people to achieve them. The more goals they achieve, the more they feel like winners. And the more they feel like winners, the more their self-esteem goes up.

Inspect what you expect. Monitor, check, and control. Once you've given a person a job, and you have been clear and specific, set performance standards and a deadline, and then, stay on top of the job.

Practice Participative Management

Participative management is a powerful tool to build involvement, commitment, loyalty, and ownership of the task. You have to believe that people need to be involved and are entitled to participate in determining the work they do, the standards that are set, and how they accomplish things. We have found over and over that the most effective work teams, especially with generations X and Y, are *democratic*, where the boss and the employees work together to in participate and discuss what needs to be done. They discuss and divide up the tasks and assign them, and then monitor and set timelines for review.

The manager should act as a coach or partner in the work. At your participative management meetings you hand out assignments, discuss work in progress, and each person hears what the others are doing. The employee's commitment to quality work is in direct proportion to their involvement in setting goals and standards. The quality of their work is going to determine your success as a manager. Quality work can never be produced without some kind of emotional commitment. Emotion and quality work are only achieved through involvement.

The Four Factors of Motivation

Motivation can be discussed in terms of four factors and three Rs. In the way you manage these factors, you show your people that you care about them. A change in any area can lead to major improvements in how people feel, and in how they perform in their jobs.

- Motivational Factor #1: *Leadership style*. This factor determines how motivated people are to perform as parts of the team. Sometimes just changing the leader changes the whole performance of the organization.
- Motivational Factor #2: *Reward structure* of the organization. In other words, what are the incentives for excellent performance? How are people paid, and what are they paid for?
- Motivational Factor #3: *Organizational climate*. Is it a happy place to work or is it a negative place to work? Is it performance-oriented place or a politically oriented place?
- Motivational Factor #4: *Structure* of the work. Some work is inherently motivational. Other work is boring or not motivating at all. This factor has a major influence on how people feel about their jobs. Good organizations are always trying to structure the work so as to match the nature of the work with the nature of the employee, to make it challenging, interesting, and personally rewarding.

Change the Leadership Style

The reward structure, the organizational climate, and the nature of the work can be changed slowly over time, but leadership style is the thing that can be changed the fastest. If you change your leadership style from negative to positive, you suddenly become a multiplying factor at work. That's why so many organizations in trouble bring in a Lee Iacocca or a Michael Eisner or another highly motivational leader. This person becomes a motivational force, affecting performance, even leaving the other three factors unchanged.

The Three Rs of Motivation

The three Rs of motivation are *rewards*, *recognition*, and *reinforcement*. Rewards can be both tangible and intangible. But they must be based solely on *performance*. The only way for a reward structure to work in motivating people to help the company to be more successful is when it is directly tied to the goals of the business. Doing a good job and making a valuable contribution is the only thing that should be rewarded. The fact is that what gets rewarded gets done. If you want to see what is getting done in an organization, just look at what's getting rewarded. When you change the structure of rewards, you immediately change behavior.

Recognition for a job well done is something that managers owe to their people. Whenever a person does something that is exceptional or even makes a good try, give them both private and public recognition. Celebrate achievement; large and small successes.

The third R in motivation is *reinforcement*. It takes place when you continually comment on, praise, and encourage good work and good behavior. What we know from behavioral psychology is that what gets reinforced gets repeated. Every time you give praise, privately and publicly, for any behavior, you are probably going to get more of it.

Successful organizations create environments where the only way you can get ahead is by contributing in specific ways to the success of the business.

Management by Values

The deepest of all human needs, right at the core of the self-concept, is the need for *meaning and purpose*. Explain how the work benefits others, especially customers, and how it contributes to their lives and work. Purpose serves as a powerful motivator. Values elicit emotional responses and deeper commitments from people.

Values such as quality, friendliness, service, respect for the individual, building self-esteem, and training and growing people are what trigger, motivate, and inspire people. But don't assume that people know what your values are. It is important that you as the manager continually reinforce your values in action. When someone is having a problem, the way you work with that person demonstrates your values. When you deal with a difficult customer, you demonstrate your true beliefs regarding customer service. When you deal with someone who is unfair or demanding, you demonstrate the values of the organization.

The Fortunate 500

Ken Blanchard and Norman Vincent Peale wrote a book together called *The Fortunate 500*. They looked at the top 20 percent of companies in each industry, those companies that had consistently achieved higher levels of profitability over multiyear periods than those in the bottom 80 percent in the same industry.

One of the distinctions they found among these companies was that all the companies had values of some kind. The difference was that the top 20 percent of the companies had *written* values that were clearly formulated and which everyone in the company knew and lived by consistently. The companies in the bottom 80 percent might have had values, but few employees knew what they were, and few were able to articulate how to live or work by those values in the daily activities of the business.

When someone joins a high-quality organization, one that is known for its values and its commitment to quality, the new person often begins to take on the thoughts, feelings, and attitudes of the new organization and to become a better and higher-performing person as a result. When a person is surrounded by winners in a corporate climate that encourages and rewards winning, he or she tends to become a high performer as well.

The Manager as Teacher

One of the most important roles that a manager has is to teach and train the people under him or her in ways to do the job better. Never make the mistake of thinking that people already know how to do their job well. If they did, they would probably not be working under you.

Taking time to teach causes people to feel valuable, and their self-esteem to go up. It makes them feel valuable and important. Take time to instruct, answer questions, and to give feedback. One of your most important responsibilities is to teach and "grow" the next generation of managers. You multiply yourself by teaching others how to do the tasks that you have already mastered.

Create a Positive Work Environment

Thousands of employees have been polled over the years to determine what they find most important and enjoyable about their work. Over and over, the same six ingredients are mentioned.

1. *Challenge.* The more challenges people experience, the more engaged they will be and the more positive they will feel about themselves. When the job is challenging, people are busy and active all day, working harder and enjoying it more.
2. *Freedom.* The more freedom people feel they have to get the job done on their own schedule and in their own way, the better they feel about themselves and their work.
3. *Control.* This factor is characterized by remaining interested and involved in the job of the subordinate. You consistently check to see how everything is going. You set regular times for review and feedback. The more sincere feedback people get on their work, the more they feel that you care about them and what they are doing.
4. *Respect.* The more you respect the employee, by asking questions, listening, and taking action on his or her ideas, the more valued and important the employee feels.
5. *Success experiences.* Give people jobs that they can perform successfully at their levels of experience and skill. The more opportunities they have to actually succeed by being given jobs that are within their capabilities, the more they feel like *winners* and the higher will be their self-esteem and self-confidence.

6. *Positive expectations*. Nothing boosts self-esteem and improves performance more than when individuals feel that a boss believes they have the capacity to do the job well.

Continuous Training and Education

An essential key to motivating your staff and showing them that you care about them and their future is to train them to become more valuable and important to both the company and to themselves. The more you invest in them, the happier they will be, the better work they will do, the more they will cooperate with each other, the more creative they will become, and the more positive a work environment you will have surrounding you.

Earl Nightingale once wrote that, "Happiness is the progressive realization of a worthy goal, or ideal." Whenever people feel that they are growing personally, becoming better and better, moving toward becoming the best person they could possibly be, they experience a continuous feeling of happiness and motivation. Nothing generates this feeling on a more consistent basis than your dedication to the continuous training, education, and development of your people. Continuous learning is the key to high performance, motivation, enthusiasm, and commitment.

The Right Question

Some managers question the idea of training their staff by asking, "What if we train them, and they leave?" But this question is not the right question. The right question is, "What if you *don't* train them, and they stay?"

Companies like IBM, Xerox in its heyday, and AT&T, are passionate about training their people on a regular basis. An employee at IBM, after several months of training prior to beginning work, was required to take 40 to 80 additional hours of training each year. It was a minimum requirement for continued employment. Such companies take training very seriously.

The best companies spend hundreds of millions of dollars each year training their people because they know that proper training has an incredibly high payoff. According to *Human Resources Executive* magazine, properly training people in the key skills of their jobs can yield 10, 20, and even 30 times the cost of the training to the bottom line in subsequent years. For every dollar that a company spends in training, they get back incredible returns on that investment.

People as the Greatest Cost

Aside from cost of goods sold, the average company's operating expenses are between 65 percent and 85 percent payroll and benefits, and only 15 percent everything else, including rent and utilities. Even including manufacturing costs, the average company spends 65 percent of its gross revenues on salaries, wages, and associated costs.

According to a study conducted by the American Society for Training and Development, average companies spend about 1 percent or less of their gross revenues on training the people who are expected to generate those revenues. According to that same study, the top 20 percent of companies in profitability in every industry spend 3 percent or more of their gross sales revenue on training their people. Some companies, those that spend as much as 5 and 10 percent of their gross sales revenues on training, consistently achieve the highest growth rates and the highest levels of profitability in their industries.

Dana Corporation, in a highly competitive market, was famous for devoting one day per week to training its people in the essential skills they needed to perform their work in an excellent fashion. As a result, they consistently outperformed and outsold their competition who worked their people five days a week and had little or no time for training.

Training and Motivation

Numerous studies have shown evidence of a direct relationship between continuous training and development, and the feeling of personal growth and increased self-esteem that people experience. Whenever an individual takes in new information and feels that more of his or her potential is being released, that individual's self-esteem goes up, and self-image improves. These individuals feel happier and more positive about themselves.

One of the jobs of management should be to develop a training plan for each staff member. Sit with the individuals and determine the skills that they will need, in addition to their existing skills, to make an increasingly more valuable contribution to the business. In a large company, you can arrange for training internally. For smaller companies, thousands of excellent training organizations are available to come in and conduct specialized training customized for your people and your business. Sometimes, one training program can completely transform the performance of an entire department or even an entire organization.

Continuous personal and professional growth is the most dependable motivator of people toward greater levels of competence and higher levels of performance. Training your people is absolutely essential to creating a winning corporate climate.

Training and Competitive Advantage

A senior executive said recently, "The only competitive advantage we have is the ability to learn and apply new ideas faster than our competitors." Just as a top sports team has a rigorous and continuous training program in place, a top company must do the same. The rule is that "your life only gets better when you get better."

By the same token, people only get better when the manager gets better. The company only gets better when staff get better. And as Pat Reilly, the basketball coach wrote, "If you're not getting better, you're getting worse." Because of the incredible speed of change and competition in every industry today, if your people and your company are not constantly improving, getting better and better, they are actually falling further and further behind those companies who are training their people to ever higher levels.

W. Edwards Deming, the quality guru said, "Training is not mandatory; neither is survival." Continuous training and development is not a choice. It is not really optional. It is a mandatory behavior for survival in the markets of today and tomorrow.

Mentoring and Motivation

Nobody does it alone. Each person who is successful today is successful as a result of the ideas, input, wisdom, and guidance of people they have met throughout their careers. Sometimes this mentoring is direct, one-on-one, in private sessions aimed at helping the individual to identify areas for improvement and to implement new ideas and skills in that area.

Sometimes mentoring is *indirect*. It comes from working with a senior person possessed of greater wisdom and experience and learning from that person by observing how he or she does a job and handles responsibilities. The best mentor I ever had personally was a senior executive who never mentored me directly at all. Instead, he let me sit in on meetings where important issues were discussed and important decisions were made. The things I learned from watching him in action still affect me today.

Take an Active Interest

One of the most powerful motivational factors in the world of work is for you to take an active interest in the careers of the people who report to you. Because you are busy, you probably do not have enough time to sit and chat with junior employees for long periods. Instead, you can be a mentor in short bursts of a few minutes or so by taking the time to give a little guidance and point them in the right direction. Individual attention from a senior person is a major motivator of personal growth and performance.

If you are serious about becoming a mentor, take the time to pick one or two people in your company and then offer to become a guide, friend, coach, and counselor to them. These individuals might be people under you or near you, or even in other departments. One of your key functions as a senior manager is to bring along young, talented, and ambitious people and to help them and guide their careers.

The wonderful thing about mentoring is that attention from a senior person whom the individual respects builds their self-esteem and self-confidence. These mentored individuals feel more important and valuable. They grow more dedicated and committed to the work and to the company.

Paying Attention Is Paying Value

According to a basic rule, whenever we pay attention to someone, we are also paying value to that person. When we pay attention, it raises another's self-esteem and it makes that person feel more important. When you pay this kind of value to junior members of your staff by taking an active interest in their lives and futures, they become more loyal and committed to you, and do a better job. Many successful executives today report that it was the effect or impact of another executive who took an interest in their progress that made all the difference in their lives and careers. It can be the same for you.

One of the greatest tributes to your success as a manager will be the number of people who say that you are the person who made them what they are today. Many senior managers find that they get their greatest satisfaction in life from following the progress of the people they have mentored over the years.

Key Considerations in Mentoring

Mentoring, however, is not as simple as selecting junior people and giving them regular advice to help them in their careers. The first consideration is always that of compatibility or chemistry. For a mentor-mentee relationship to work, the two must be relaxed and comfortable with each other.

I have sought out mentors in the past, and at the first meeting, realized it was not a good fit. The other person and I did not get along in a comfortable, relaxed fashion. It was soon clear to both of us that we were not headed toward a good mentor-mentee relationship.

People have approached me to be their mentor in the past as well. In some cases, I have been a mentor to those people for months and even years. In other cases, after the first meeting, the lack of rapport between us was clear, and the mentor relationship never got off the ground.

Take Your Time

If you are seeking a mentor-mentee relationship with a person above you, start with a cup of coffee and explain to the person that you would much appreciate their occasional input and guidance in your career. If they are open to this relationship and the two of you are compatible, be sure that you do not overwhelm the other person with time demands. Keep your mentoring sessions to approximately 10 minutes.

When you meet with your mentor, have a list of questions, concerns, or observations that you would like to discuss. Be sure that you have a copy for your mentor. When your mentor gives you recommendations of books to read or courses to take, be sure to take action on those recommendations immediately. Report back to your mentor what you did and what you learned. This behavior will reinforce to your mentor that spending time with you is a good investment in the future.

Instruct Your Mentee

When you become a mentor, explain these general rules and guidelines for effective mentoring to the other person. Have them come to you with a written list of questions or concerns. Schedule your meetings in 10-minute blocks, or longer if you have the time. Have a specific starting and stopping time. Be punctual for the meeting, and end the meeting at the time agreed.

Parkinson's Law says that "Work expands to fill the time allotted for it." If you allocate 10 or 15 minutes to a mentoring session, and the mentee is aware of that, you will be happily surprised at how quickly you get through all the items on the list in that short period of time.

Both being a mentor and being a mentee can be greatly enriching experiences in your life. As you mentor junior staff, you can often have an influence on them that will last for many years, if not their entire lifetimes.

Leading by Example

One of the most important responsibilities of management is to lead by example and to be a *role model* for your staff. In this way, you help them shape their personal self-ideals by being the kind of person that they admire and respect. Leading by example is an absolute requirement in management and a prerequisite for leadership. The level of character and performance among people in the workplace can never be higher or better than the behaviors, standards, and integrity of the management, including yourself.

You do not *raise* moral levels in an organization. Morals filter down from the top. They are based on the character and personality of the leader or manager. The words and actions of the manager set the tone of the entire department whether positive or negative, productive or unproductive.

The Great Question

One of the great questions for you to ask is: "What kind of company would my company be if everyone in it was just like me?" In business, staff generally treat customers the way they are treated by their managers. Whenever you experience excellent customer service, you know that the manager behind the scenes takes good care of his or her people. Whenever you experience poor customer service, you know these people report to a poor or negative manager. Because they cannot pay their manager back for the negative way they are being treated, they simply take it out on the customers. You see this behavior often.

The key is for you to adopt a warm, friendly, and supportive personality with your people. You create a positive corporate climate by being a positive, cheerful, and confident person yourself. Emotions are contagious. At work, the boss and everything he or she does have an inordinate influence on the thoughts, feelings, attitudes, and behaviors of the staff. A positive or encouraging word from the boss can make a person feel happy and more productive all day long. On the other hand, a negative comment or a frown from the boss can cause a person to feel anxious, insecure, and generally less productive for the rest of the day. The things that you do and say as a manager have an inordinate impact on other people.

Everyone Is Watching

Everybody watches the boss, all the time. They watch you out of the corners of their eye. Whatever you say to anyone is quickly relayed to everyone else. And *everyone knows everything*. There are no secrets in a business or an organization. If you make a positive or negative comment about someone, even casually, it will speed back to that person faster than you can imagine, and usually distorted from what you actually said.

One of the best ways to lead by example is to always be *positive*. Always speak in a positive and uplifting way about each staff member when you are talking to other staff members. Whenever you compliment workers outside of their earshot, that comment will get back to them quite quickly and have the desired effect of raising their self-esteem and improving their self-image.

In meetings, you are on display. Everyone is watching you. They are watching and aware of everything you do or say, and even the things that you neglect to do or say.

The Testing Time

The most important time for you to set an example is when things go *wrong*, when you are under pressure, when a major problem, reversal, or setback occurs in the organization. This "testing time" is when and where you need to demonstrate the real quality of your character. These moments are when you show everyone who you really are inside.

In 2010, I was diagnosed with throat cancer. For someone who has built a 20-person business around professional speaking, seminars, and audio/video recordings, the discovery that I had throat cancer was a real shock. At the same time, I realized all of my staff would be affected by my diagnosis. Because people think about their incomes continually, they would especially wonder whether their jobs were safe and secure. Fortunately, I had excellent doctors, and the cancer was one that was eminently treatable. My doctors had caught it at *stage 1*, and although it required chemotherapy, surgery, and radiation to deal with it, I was not in any danger of losing my life.

As soon as I understood the gravity, or lack of gravity of my situation, I made it a regular habit to go into my office and talk to each person on a weekly basis. I remained continually positive, upbeat, and cheerful. I told them what was going on, my course of treatment, what was likely to happen, when I would lose my voice and for how long, and every other detail. As a result, although staff members were worried, they continued to be positive and to carry on the business of the company as though everything was quite normal.

An Opportunity to Demonstrate Character

Whenever you have a problem or a crisis in your business, remember that everyone is watching you. In such a situation, you have an opportunity to demonstrate your qualities and character as a leader. Your job is not to react to negative situations, but to respond calmly and effectively, and to keep everybody focused on solutions and on doing a good job.

As the leader, if you want other people to be effective, efficient, and punctual, you must also be effective, efficient, and punctual. Manage your time well. Set clear priorities, work on your most important tasks, and demonstrate diligence and industriousness at your work for all to see. You cannot expect other people to perform at any higher level than you perform on a day-to-day basis.

As the manager, be courageous and decisive. Be willing to take principled positions, stand up for your staff, make firm decisions, and be able to explain the reasons for the things you do. Just imagine that every day and in every way your staff are watching you and forming their own behaviors by observing the way you act. Set a good example for them so that if they all behave the way you do, your company would be a terrific place to work.

Listen to Your Staff

Leaders are listeners. Leaders listen twice as much as they talk. The best leaders have a high question-to-talk ratio. They ask a lot of questions of their staff and give them an opportunity to express themselves openly and honestly on a regular basis.

You can tell the quality of the relationship between the manager and the employee by how freely the employee feels in expressing his or her ideas and opinions to the manager without fear of being criticized or ignored. The employee trusts that his or her comments will be heard.

In the annual studies of www.agreatplacetowork.com, one of the most important characteristics of the best companies is that they have high levels of *trust*. Trust is defined as "I can speak my opinions freely to my manager without fear of being criticized or losing my job."

Listening Is Powerful

Listening has been called "white magic" because of its almost magical effect on building up people and making them feel terrific about themselves. When you listen to another person, you "pay value" to that other person and make them feel more important and worthwhile.

The average manager spends 60 percent or more of his or her time in meetings and conversation with staff members and superiors. The more and the better you listen, the more aware you will be of what is going on. The faster you will sense problems or difficulties that you can help to resolve. The more you listen, the more relaxed and confident will be your people in your presence.

Four Keys to Effective Listening

First: Listen Attentively

Lean forward and listen closely to what the other person is saying. Put aside all distractions. Turn off your computer and mute your telephone. When you sit and talk with a staff member, treat that person as if they are the most important person in the world.

Dale Carnegie once said, "Rapt attention is the highest form of flattery." When you listen intently to another person, it affects them physically. Their heart rate increases. Their galvanic skin response goes up. Their blood pressure increases. When you listen intently to another person, making them feel more valuable and important, their self-esteem and self-confidence go up as well.

Rapt attention means leaning forward, looking at the person's face intently, and flicking your eyes occasionally to their eyes. Nodding and smiling are also parts of being an *active* listener. Let others know that what they are saying is important to you and that you are paying close attention to it.

Most of all, do not interrupt or even attempt to interrupt. Most people are so concerned with their next comment that they barely listen to the other. They merely wait for an opportunity to jump in when the other person takes a breath.

Second: Pause Before Replying

When the other person stops talking, instead of immediately commenting, allow a silence to develop in the conversation. It need not be more than three to five seconds, but a brief silence gives you three advantages:

1. When you pause, you tell the other person that you are carefully considering what they've said, which makes them feel more valuable and respected.
2. When you pause, you avoid the risk of interrupting the other person if they are just reorganizing their thoughts before continuing.
3. When you pause, you actually hear the other person's meaning at a deeper level of mind. Remember, it is not only what the person says, but what they *don't* say that is essential to the message they are conveying.

The best listeners practice the "art of the pause" in every conversation. It gives them a tremendous advantage in both understanding and in being understood.

Third: Question for Clarification

Never assume what the person really means by what they are saying. Instead, if you sense any ambiguity, simply ask, "How do you mean?" This question is the most powerful of all questions for guiding and directing a conversation.

People are conditioned from early childhood to respond whenever they are asked a question. When you ask the question "How do you mean?" the individual will almost invariably answer by expanding on his or her previous comments, giving you more material to enable you to understand clearly what he or she really means.

Remember, *the person who asks questions has control.* The person answering the questions is controlled by the person who is asking the questions. The more questions you ask, the more control you have over the conversation in a positive way. The more you ask questions, the more you learn and understand. Having more information enables you to make better decisions and to be a better manager.

Fourth: Paraphrase the Speaker's Words

Feed back what the person has just said, and paraphrase it in your own words. This "acid test" of listening is where you demonstrate that you *really* were listening closely to what the other person was saying, rather than smiling politely while being preoccupied with your own thoughts.

You can say something such as, "Let me make sure I understand exactly where you're coming from . . ." and then go on to rephrase what the other person has just said. When the other person agrees that, yes, you really understand what he or she trying to say, you can then reply with your own comments or observations.

Ask Questions

Asking questions is the key to leadership and to good communications. When you ask questions, you get a chance to listen to the answers. And listening builds trust.

Trust between two people is the foundation of peak performance. Even more important, listening builds *character*. The more you listen to other people and genuinely try to understand and empathize with them, the more you develop yourself. This development comes out of the tremendous discipline that is required to listen attentively without interrupting. Practice listening patiently in an unhurried and relaxed way. Listen as if you have all the time in the world. Remember that some people need more time to get to the point than others.

Listening also enables you to get a real understanding of what your people are thinking and feeling. When people feel that they can speak openly and honestly to their boss, and their boss focuses his or her entire attention on attempting to understand what they are saying, the boss is conveying value to those employees, expressing care about them, and saying he or she considers them to be important. Listening to other people is a powerful motivational tool that not only builds them up, but it also builds you up, and makes you a better and better-informed manager.

Practice the Friendship Factor

When employees were asked in a recent survey the characteristics of the best bosses they had ever had, they almost universally replied by saying, "I always felt as though the boss cared about me as a person, rather than just as a member of the staff."

The friendship factor is the most important relationship quality that leads to and enables people to perform at their very best. Establishing high levels of friendship among the staff and between the staff and the manager is the key to success in business today. The quality of the interaction between the employer and employees is the vital determinant of motivation and performance in any organization.

The existence or nonexistence of the friendship factor is what will determine how helpful your staff will be, and how cooperative they are when it comes to working together with you and the other team members to get the job done. In a larger sense, it is safe to say that your success in business is going to be proportional to the number and quality of business friendships that you develop throughout your career. It is not just the number of people you know, but the number of people who know you in a positive way. The more that people know you and like you, the more open they will be to voluntarily helping you in your life and work.

The existence of the friendship factor has a huge impact on whether your employees will perform at a higher level or quality, achieve excellence, and feel terrific about themselves when working with you.

Practice Clarity and Consideration

Excellent managers seem to have a balance of two important qualities—clarity and consideration. They express caring, concern, and compassion with their employees, treating them like members of their corporate family, and making them feel happy and secure in their work. At the same time, they are absolutely crystal clear with regard to tasks, outputs, and the responsibilities of each person. Each person knows exactly what is expected of him or her to do their job well.

The friendship factor is developed with the three Cs: consideration, caring, and courtesy. These behaviors toward the people who report to them are the norm for excellent managers. You practice *consideration* with your staff when you ask them about themselves, and especially about their families and their personal lives. When you show an interest in what they are doing *outside* of work, you tell them better than any other way that you value them as individuals who have lives that are separate and apart from the work place. When you ask people about their personal lives, and listen attentively to the answers, they feel more valuable and important, and as a result they like and respect you even more.

Care About Your Staff

You express *caring* about your staff members when they tell you of a problem and you immediately stop and make an effort to help them to solve the problem in some way. For example, with my staff, I always tell them that, "Children come first." By this comment, I mean that if ever their child has a need or problem of any kind while they are at work, they can leave immediately to take care of their child without any deduction of pay or requirement to make up the time. For young mothers, it is one of the very best ways to show that you really care for them and the most important parts of their lives.

When you ask them questions about their family and their personal life, listen attentively, and express sympathy for the challenges they face, you demonstrate that you genuinely care. You also show caring and consideration by being appreciative and complimenting them on their possessions, clothes, and their personal achievements.

Practice Golden Rule Management

You express courtesy toward your staff when you show personal regard and respect for each person. When you maintain a courteous demeanor, especially under stress when a situation goes wrong or when an employee has a problem, you increase your people's feelings of security and comfort in the workplace. When you are courteous to people, it leads to improved morale and higher motivation.

The key to the friendship factor is for you to practice what is called "Golden Rule Management." Treat other people the way you would like to be treated by your superiors. Treat your staff like partners and clients and as essential, valued parts of the enterprise.

When Jack Welch was president of General Electric, he encouraged all managers to treat their staff as though their staff members would be managers over them the following year. Because of the dynamic structure of General Electric and the rapid promotion of highly competent people, it was not uncommon for a person to find themselves working under a person who had been under them not long ago. This potential change of positions caused everyone in General Electric to treat each other exactly as they would want to be treated if the roles were reversed.

The Best Time of
Your Work Life

The best time of your work life is when are getting along the best with your boss. The worst time in your work life is when you are having difficulties or problems with your boss. Your job as a manager is to make sure that you are getting along well with everyone and that they are all getting along well with you.

It is quite easy for you to practice the Golden Rule in your behavior toward your staff. You can simply ask yourself, "What causes me to feel the best about myself when I am at work? Who are the best bosses I have ever had, and what did they do or say to me that made me feel happy about my work?" Whatever your answers to these questions, use them as guides to the way you treat your own staff.

What makes you happy, excited, enthusiastic, and fulfilled at work? How can you create this same positive feeling among the people who report to you? What is the ideal relationship that you would like to have with your co-workers? Do and say the same things to other people that you would want them to do and say to you, if the positions were reversed.

The more time you take to tell and show your people that they are valuable and important, and that you care about them, the better manager you will be and the better results you will get.

Action Exercises

1. Identify your most valuable people, the ones on whom you depend the most. What could you do right now to show them that your care about them?

2. Treat your staff each day as if you would be working under them one year from today. What would you do differently?

3. Practice the three Rs of motivation each day—rewards, recognition, and reinforcement. Tell people on a regular basis how good they are.

4. Show your staff that you care about them by asking them questions about their personal and family lives, and by taking a genuine interest in them.

5. Practice active listening with your staff when they want to talk. Pay attention, don't interrupt, and ask questions for clarification.

6. Select one or two of your high-potential staff members and look for ways to mentor and guide them to be more successful.

7. Identify key skills that your staff members could learn that would make them more valuable to the company and to themselves. Help and encourage them to acquire these skills.

CHAPTER TEN

THE DISCIPLINE OF CHANGE MANAGEMENT

*"Survival goes not to the strongest or most intelligent of
the species, but to the one most adaptable to change."*
—Charles Darwin

Your success as a leader will be largely determined by how efficiently
and effectively you respond to the challenges of change in your business. Change is inevitable, unavoidable, unstoppable, and mostly
unpredictable. The better you are with dealing with the incredible speed
of change in your business and personal life, the greater your contribution will be and the more valuable you will be to your organization.

Three major factors drive change today: information explosion,
technology expansion, and determined competition. Let's take each
one of these in order.

Information Explosion

The amount of information available today is greater than at any other
time in human history, and it is multiplying at a faster rate than ever
before. In 1980, about 220,000 new books were published each year
in the United States. In 2013, more than 3 million new books will be
published, plus millions of articles on every conceivable subject.

One new idea or piece of information generated by someone,
somewhere on the planet, can create a new business or industry, or

render an existing industry obsolete. When Apple introduced the iPhone in 2006, it was dismissed by the people at RIM (BlackBerry), the world leader in business cell phones, as a toy. In their wisdom, they concluded that it would never interfere with their business of producing complex cell phones with highly secure algorithms for business use.

Today, BlackBerry's two presidents have left the company, sales are down 80 percent, and it is doubtful that the company will be able to develop a new phone that will enable it to survive in the years ahead. The entire game has changed.

Fully 90 percent of the best thinkers, scientists, writers, creators, and entrepreneurs who have ever lived in human history are living and working today. The smartest, brightest, most creative, and determined scientists and researchers who have ever lived are working right now to discover new ideas and applications that can be used to improve products and services of all kinds, and to develop new ones.

Technology Expansion

The rule of thumb is that any new high-tech product is probably obsolete before it reaches the market. By the time it is developed, manufactured, packaged, and distributed to customers, the company or a competitor is already developing something that is better, faster, or cheaper, and racing it to the marketplace. The saying goes that "If it works, it's obsolete."

Changes in information technology and distribution can be devastating to old-line companies. Within a year of Apple's introduction of the iPad, which, in conjunction with Kindle and others, enabled people to download books in seconds, rather than travelling across town to visit a bookstore, the whole industry had changed. Within 12 months, one of the biggest and most successful brick-and-mortar book chains in the world, Borders, went bankrupt, closing 600 stores forever. E-book sales jumped to more than 50 percent of the market in 2012, and continue to grow. The entire world of book publishing has been shaken up dramatically with no one in the industry knowing exactly what is going to happen next with advances in technology.

The Growth of Competition

The third factor driving change today is competition. More businesses, individuals, and organizations are competing today to get the customer's dollar than ever before. Today, an entrepreneur with a laptop, sitting at home in his bedroom, can start an international marketing, sales, and distribution business for a few dollars and are now doing so—by the *millions*. By December 2012, more than 1 million engineers and entrepreneurs in the United States alone were working to develop the next "killer app" for the smartphone. This number is greater than the entire farm population working in the country today.

If you have children today, when they grow up, they will probably be working for a company that does not now exist, producing and selling products and services that do not now exist, selling to customers and markets that do not now exist, and selling against competition that does not now exist. Fully 80 percent of the products and services that will be in common use five years from now do not exist today either.

The formula is simple: IE × TE × CO = ROC (information explosion multiplied by technological expansion multiplied by competition equals the rate of change). Because all three of these factors are increasing, the rate of change in five years will be beyond our imaginations. You will experience more changes in one year than your parents or grandparents experienced in their entire lifetimes. And if anything, the rate of change is accelerating faster and faster.

Predictions from Harvard

Harvard University made three predictions about change. First, they said more *change* in your field or business would take place in the coming year than ever before. Second, more *competition* will be part of your business or industry in the coming year than ever before. Third, more *opportunities* will happen in your business or industry, but they will be different from what you are doing today.

These predictions were made in 1952. An additional prediction was made shortly thereafter. They concluded that fully 72 percent of people working today will be in completely different jobs within two years unless they learn to adapt to change and turn it to their advantage.

Your Most Important Work

The most important and valuable work that you do consists of "thinking." The quality of your thinking determines the quality of your life. Your ability to think clearly and well about change, and how you are going to deal with it, is a vital part of leadership at any level of the organization.

Your job is to become a *master* of change rather than a *victim* of change. Your goal is to accept the inevitability of change and use change to your advantage. Your ability to change faster than your competitors in the face of new information, new advances in technology, and different customer demands is the key to your surviving and thriving in the future.

The starting point of dealing with change effectively is for you to *expect* it to happen in a continuous and unpredictable way. Many negative emotions are caused by "frustrated expectations." You expect things to work out in a particular way and they do not; they disappoint you. But if you expect change as an inevitable and unavoidable fact of life, you will be much more relaxed and effective in dealing with change when it comes, even though you cannot predict the form or timing with any great accuracy.

Remain Flexible

The Menninger Institute did a study in the 1990s to determine the most important quality for success in business in the twenty-first century. They concluded that the most important quality that you could develop would be that of "flexibility." With flexibility, like the willow in a storm, you would bend with the realities of change rather than breaking or becoming angry or upset.

The discipline of change management requires that you apply zero-based thinking to every part of your business on a regular basis. With zero-based thinking, like zero-based accounting, you draw a line under all of your previous decisions and put them on trial for their lives. You ask this question: "What am I doing that, knowing what I now know, I would not start up again today if I had to do it over?"

We call this a KWINK analysis. Knowing what I now know, what am I doing today that I would not get into again today if I had the chance to do it over?

Cut Your Losses

Zero-based thinking needs to be applied in three areas: issues that involve time, money, and investments. People hate to *lose* anything and will go to almost any measure to prevent a loss. Many people invest an enormous amount of time in a product, service, project, or even a person, and hate to admit that knowing what they now know, it was not a good investment of time. But remember, whatever time you have invested in a person or project in the past, it is a sunk cost now. It is irretrievable. It is gone forever.

One of the best strategies for dealing with rapid change is for you to "cut your losses" when you realize you have made a mistake and invested a lot of time in something that, in retrospect, was not a good use of time. Have the courage and the willingness to cut it off and turn your attention to something with greater potential.

The second type of investment has to do with money. Again, most financial investments are sunk costs. They cannot be retrieved; the money is gone forever. It seemed like a good idea at the time, but it didn't work out. Let it go, and move on.

The third area has to do with emotions. Many people invest an enormous amount of emotion in a relationship, a career, a company, or a product or service. Even when these activities are not successful, the natural tendency is to hold onto them, rather than accepting that they did not work out and move on instead.

Zero-based thinking is one of the most helpful thinking tools ever discovered. It frees your mind and opens you up to all the possibilities of the future, rather than keeping you locked into the decisions and commitments that did not work out in the past.

Walk Across the Street

In developing the discipline of change management, you should use the "walk-across-the-street method" and apply it to both your business and your career. Imagine that your company burned to the ground, but all your people managed to escape safely to the parking lot. Then imagine that offices or facilities are available across the street for you to move into immediately and get your business up and running as quickly as possible.

If you were going to walk across the street and start your business anew, what would you begin to do immediately? What products and services would you immediately want to begin producing for your market? Who are the markets and customers that you would immediately want to contact and become active with? If you were starting your business over again today, what products, processes, services, markets, and other activities would you not start up again today?

Finally, if you were walking across the street to start your business again, which of your staff would you bring with you to the new business, and which of them would you leave in the parking lot?

This way of thinking is how you reinvent yourself and your business on a regular basis. You imagine that you have *no limitations* and that you can start again right where you are, with no baggage from the past. What would you do differently?

Practice Crisis Anticipation

An important aspect of managing change is for you to *anticipate* it. Look down the road into the future and ask yourself, "What are the worst things that could happen that would change or disrupt my business, or threaten its survival?"

Your ability to think into the future, and to accurately anticipate the problems that could occur, is a mark of the superior executive. This *extrapolatory thinking* is like playing ahead down the chessboard of life. What moves could you take? What moves are your competitors likely to take? And what would you do then?

Royal Dutch Shell (RDS) is famous for its "scenario planning division." Its experts have developed more than 600 scenarios for disruptive events that could occur all around the world in the business of extracting and shipping oil, moving tankers or platforms to various countries and refineries, producing oil products and distributing them to consumers, and every other aspect of the business. For example, if a war erupts somewhere in the Middle East, RDS has a scenario all planned, developed, and ready to implement within 24 hours. If a tsunami happens in Japan, RDS has a scenario to deal with that event. As a result of its ability to think well into the future and to anticipate what might happen, RDS is consistently one of the most successful and profitable companies in the world. It is seldom affected for long when disruptions of any kind occur in any of their markets or activities.

Identify the Worst Possible Outcome

Here is an exercise for you: Look down the road one, two, or three years and ask yourself, "What are the worst things that could happen which could seriously disrupt our existing business?" And then, in this exercise, use the "Three Percent Rule." This rule says that if the probability of a negative event occurring is 3 percent or greater, you should consider it as a possible future reality and think about what you would do if it occurred. Remember, you are only as free as your well-developed *options*. What options could you develop to protect yourself if a major negative event were to happen?

Think about changes in information or technology and, especially, your competition. Remember, hope is not a plan, and wishing is not an option. We spoke earlier about the importance of a long time perspective. Your ability to project your thinking forward into the future and to look around you, anticipating the worst possible things that could go wrong, is essential in any leadership role. You then look back to the present situation, and think about the specific steps you could today take to guard against these potential negative outcomes or to minimize the damage from them.

Practice the Tip of the Iceberg Principle

Another way to develop the discipline of change management is for you to prepare for the inevitable and unavoidable changes that are coming. In the "tip of the iceberg" principle, when something happens in your business or industry that is unusual and unexpected, instead of dismissing it as a single event, you assume in advance that it is the tip of an iceberg. It is an indicator of a trend in your business that you must anticipate and take provisions to guard against or take advantage of.

Identify the Skills and Competencies You Will Need

What knowledge, skills, abilities, and competencies are you going to need in the future to be a leader in your industry? What are your plans to begin developing these capacities well in advance? What people, resources, products, services, and technologies will you need to become an industry leader? Where and how are you going to acquire them?

Michael Kami, the strategic planner, said "The best way to predict the future is to create it." Once you have settled on a long-term business goal, you ask these three questions regularly:

1. What additional knowledge and skills will we require to achieve this goal?
2. What are the major obstacles we will have to overcome to achieve this goal?
3. Whose support and cooperation will we need to achieve this goal?

Preparation is the mark of the professional. There is no such thing as the word *overprepare* in the vocabulary of top leaders. Sometimes your anticipation of one key detail or event can have a major impact on your business. When you experience a major change in your business, call a time-out, like in a football game, and stop the ball. Take some time to analyze the change that has taken place carefully and thoughtfully before you react or overreact to it.

Dealing with Death and Disaster

A major change in business is much like the phenomenon of death in a family. Elizabeth Kübler-Ross, the psychologist who taught about the process of dealing with death, said that each person goes through a series of stages before getting back to normal after a death in the family. In addition, to Kübler-Ross's five stages, the business changes encompass two more stages.

- Stage 1: *Denial.* "This can't be happening!" Whenever you experience a sudden and unexpected reversal, your natural tendency is to deny that it is happening in the first place.
- Stage 2: *Anger.* "How could this happen? Why did it occur?"
- Stage 3: *Blame.* "Who is responsible? Who did it? Let's go on a witch hunt."
- Stage 4: *Bargaining.* At this point you try to minimize the damage, to explain away the negative consequences, and to look for ways to avoid the reality of what has happened.
- Stage 5: *Depression.* You finally accept that the event has occurred. It is nonreversible. It is over. The market has collapsed. The product has failed. The money has been lost.
- Stage 6: *Acceptance.* In this first positive stage, you finally realize that it has happened and that it is now an event in the past. It can't be changed. The time, money, or emotion has been lost irrevocably. The only choice, really, is to pull yourself together and move forward.

- Stage 7: *Resurgence.* In this final stage, you resolve to take action and move forward aggressively toward your next goal or challenge. You put the negative event behind you and focus on the future.

Everyone goes through these stages when they experience a setback or reversal of any kind. The only question is: "How long does it take you to move through these stages?" Top leaders are capable of moving through these stages quite quickly, sometimes in just a few minutes, to come out the other side into acceptance and resurgence, and then get on with the business of dealing with the future.

Correlation versus Causation

In analyzing something that has happened, resist the temptation to confuse correlation with causation. Many people tend to commit this major thinking error. They assume that if two events occur at the same time, one event caused the other, which is often not the case. But if you assume that one event caused the other, you could immediately become angry or even confused. The decisions and actions that you take can be completely wrong. Therefore, it is important that you take time to think through the event and make sure of the exact reasons why it occurred without making any assumptions in advance.

Resist the Tendency to Catastrophize

In analyzing something that has happened, avoid the tendency toward "catastrophizing," thinking about or assuming the worst in a particular event. It is said that nothing is ever as *bad* as it seems, and nothing is ever as *good* as it seems. Most events fall in the grey area, rather than being black or white. In analyzing something that has happened, an unexpected change, ask as many questions as possible.

Keep Control with Questions

By asking rather than just reacting angrily, you remain calm and in control of the situation.

Ask questions such as:

1.   What exactly has happened?
2.   How did it happen?
3.   Who is involved in this situation?
4.   What are the possible costs or ramifications of this change?
5.   What are the various courses of actions available to us?
6.   What are all the possible solutions?
7.   Is this change really a problem?
8.   Could this unexpected change be an opportunity for us to do something differently?
9.   Is this change a fact or a problem? Can anything be done about this situation or is it a new reality that cannot be changed?
10.   What actions should we take immediately to deal with this change?

Get the Facts

The final part of dealing effectively with an unexpected change is for you to get the facts. Get the real facts. Not the assumed facts or the probable facts. Check your information. Then, double-check your information to be sure that what you think has happened has actually happened. As Ronald Reagan said, "Trust, but verify."

It is amazing how often people overreact to what they consider to be bad news without first checking to find out if what they have heard is true. In many cases, it is not. In many cases, the reality is quite different from what you may have heard. Take the time to ask questions and to do your homework before you make a decision.

Seek the Valuable Lesson

If a change has occurred, and it cannot be remedied or reversed, take advantage of it. Instead of thinking of it as a problem, think of it as a challenge or an opportunity. Napoleon Hill was famous for saying "Within every problem or difficulty lies the seed of an equal or greater benefit or advantage."

Often, when a change takes place in your business, it contains within it an opportunity and even the necessity of doing something completely different, something that may benefit your business in the future. Seek the valuable lesson in every problem or difficulty you face, and you will almost always find it.

Growth Is the Law of Life

Growth is the law of life, and change is the law of growth. It is not possible for you to rise to greater heights except by recognizing and taking advantage of the endless and continuous flow of the changes taking place in your life. One of my favorite reminders is "Problems come not to obstruct, but to instruct."

Tony Robbins says, "There is no such thing as failure; there is only feedback." Because you cannot reverse a change that has taken place, your best course of action is to seek ways to benefit from it. Look for ways to turn it to your personal or corporate advantage. Sometimes the greatest breakthroughs in business come about as the result of a completely unanticipated change in competitive behavior, consumer demands, or the fast-changing marketplace. If a change has occurred and cannot be reversed, your next step is to accept it as a reality.

Practice detachment when something has happened that you can't change. Accepting a fact as reality is the first step to moving on beyond the change or setback toward the real goals of building your business. The inability to get over a bad situation or setback is a major block that holds people back from happiness and long-term success.

You Are Not a Victim

If a change has taken place, and it cannot be reversed, simply accept it and move on. You are not a victim. Don't waste a minute feeling sorry for yourself. Just get so busy working on your goals that you don't have time to worry about what has happened, especially if it cannot be changed.

Another way to deal with change effectively is for you to take responsibility for it. The source of personal power in dealing with change is for you to accept 100 percent responsibility and to take charge, rather than becoming angry or upset, or blaming other people. Leaders take responsibility for problems and difficulties. They give away the praise and accolades for successes to others. Just say those magic words, "I am responsible," and then focus on the *solution*— on what can be done, rather than on the past and what cannot be changed.

The key is to put the situation behind you and focus all of your time and attention on what can be done, rather than on what has already happened. In the Marine Corps, they teach both the officers and enlisted a mantra in basic training; "Adapt! Adjust! Respond!" Your personal ability to adapt, adjust, and respond effectively to the inevitable and unavoidable changes that you will experience at an ever-increasing speed and level of unpredictability is the mark of the superior leader.

Three Enemies of Change

The three major enemies of change are the comfort zone, learned helplessness, and the path of least resistance. The comfort zone is perhaps the greatest enemy of human success. It is the natural tendency of people to become comfortable doing what they are doing, no matter what is happening around them, and then to resist the need or demand for change of any kind, even beneficial change.

Rejecting New Product Ideas

One of the major examples of this striving to stay within a comfort zone in a business is the rejection of any new product, service, or technology that might take away or cannibalize the existing products or services. It is amazing how many companies have great ideas for new products or services that are promptly squashed by senior management because if the new product or service became popular, the sales of their existing products would be affected.

Kodak Corporation scientists developed the first digital camera back in 1986. When they took it upstairs to the senior decision makers, they were told quite bluntly that, "Kodak is a film company." The scientists were told to go back downstairs and discontinue their work on this radical new technology that would or could eat into their film sales. Kodak is today bankrupt because they were too comfortable with their success in the film industry to be open to the possibilities of digital photography for the future.

This example shows why many product and service breakthroughs come from upstarts, young companies from outside the industry who have no "legacy issues." They are not in a comfort zone. In fact they are distinctly *uncomfortable* and driven to produce new products and services to survive and thrive in a competitive market.

Nokia dominated the world of cell phones for a full decade. The Nokia engineers came up with both the one-button cell phone, that could hold additional applications and serve almost as a mini-computer, as well as the tablet computer, that is currently manufactured by Apple. In both cases, the engineers took these technological breakthroughs to senior people for approval. In both cases, they were told to go back to their laboratory and stop working on a product that might interfere with Nokia's traditional cell phone business. Apple piggybacked on these concepts, developed their own technology, brought out the iPhone and the iPad, and totally transformed the world of cell phones and tablet technology.

Learned Helplessness

The second major obstacle to change is called "learned helplessness," which is what happens when an individual or organization sees the effects of rapid change in the marketplace and feels helpless to adapt or adjust to them. Without giving it much thought, many people think they lack the time, money, or ability to keep current with the technological advances of their competitors. They instead make excuses and try to hide behind their existing products and technologies rather than recognize that their markets are changing dramatically and that their customers are demanding newer, better, faster, cheaper, and easier-to-use products and services.

BlackBerry is a perfect example of this "head-in-the-sand" attitude of learned helplessness. When the Apple iPhone was released, they looked at the incredible advances in technology contained in the iPhone and just turned away. They felt that there was no way they could compete with this phone, and besides, they convinced themselves that they didn't have to. It was just a passing fad. Meanwhile, Samsung of Korea recognized that the entire world of cell phones had changed and immediately began developing the Android operating system. In cooperation with Google, they leaped the Apple wave and are now the world's leading suppliers of smartphones, complete with features and applications that no one even dreamed of five years ago.

The Path of Least Resistance

The third enemy of change is the "path of least resistance." This natural tendency leads individuals to seek faster, easier ways to get the things they want, and to simultaneously avoid the hard and difficult activities necessary to succeed in a competitive market.

Everything worthwhile in business is difficult. It requires tremendous commitments of time, money, and energy, usually extended over a long period of time. It requires hard, dedicated work, with no guarantees of success. For this reason, business leaders have developed the discipline of hard work, the willingness to put in far more hours and efforts than the average person to assure that they survive and thrive in rapidly changing competitive times.

The discipline of managing change is one of the most important qualities that you can develop to lead your field in the exciting months and years ahead. By adjusting, adapting, and responding rapidly to the unavoidable changes taking place in your business and in your personal world, you give yourself an incredible advantage that will, as much as anything, assure your survival and success in the years ahead.

Action Exercises

1. Identify the three most important information changes that can affect your sales and profitability in the future. What can you do about them?

2. Identify the three most important changes taking place in technology that can affect your business. What can you do to adapt to them?

3. Identify the three most important competitive changes taking place in your industry. How can you take advantage of them?

4. What are the worst things that could happen to disrupt your business in the next year? What steps could you take to guard against them happening?

5. What is it that you are doing in your business or personal life that, knowing what you now know, you wouldn't get into again today? How can you get out, and how fast?

6. Imagine walking across the street and starting your business or career over again. What would you do differently?

7. Identify three competencies that you or your company will need to survive and thrive in the years ahead. What is your plan to acquire them?

CHAPTER ELEVEN

THE DISCIPLINE OF CONCENTRATION

*"The key to successful time management is doing
the most important task first, and giving it your full
concentration, to the exclusion of everything else."*
—Alex MacKenzie

Your ability to manage your time, as much as any other practice in your career as an executive, will determine your success or failure. Time is the one indispensable and irreplaceable resource of accomplishment. It is your most precious asset. It cannot be saved, nor can it be recovered once lost. Everything you have to do requires time; and the better you use your time, the more you will accomplish, and the greater will be your rewards.

Time management is essential to maximum health and personal effectiveness. How much you feel in control of your time and your life is a major determinant of your level of inner peace, harmony, and mental well-being. A feeling of being "out of control" of your time is the major source of stress, anxiety, and unhappiness. The better you can organize and control the critical events of your life, the better you will feel, moment to moment, the more energy you will have, the better you will sleep, and the more you will get done.

The Four Ds

For you to accomplish anything worthwhile, including becoming excellent at time and personal management, requires four key elements:

- The first D is *desire*; you must have an intense, burning desire to get your time under control and to achieve maximum effectiveness.
- The second D is *decision*; you must make a clear decision that you are going to practice good time management techniques until they become a habit.
- The third D is *determination*; you must be willing to persist in the face of all temptations to the contrary until you have become an effective time manager. Your desire will reinforce your determination.
- The fourth, and the most important key to success in life, is *discipline*. You must discipline yourself to make time management a lifelong practice. Discipline is the ability to make yourself do what you know you should do, when you should do it, whether you feel like it or not.

The Key to High Achievement

The payoff for becoming an excellent time manager is huge. The ability to get *results* is the most outwardly identifiable quality of a top performer in any field. In its simplest terms, highly productive people use their time well. Poor performers use their time poorly.

Fortunately, all time manageable skills are *learnable*. You can develop the habits of time management that you need to enable you to be one of the most productive and highest performing people in your field. The key is to "Form good habits and make them your masters." Once you form your good habits, they will then form you and determine the direction of your career.

Success in life, in general, is quite *rare*. Success in business is rarer still. Less than 5 percent of men and women who go into the world of business ever fulfill their true potential. The reason behind this statistic is simple: they do not use their time properly. Time management is the essential skill of success in business and in life.

Time management is really life management. It is the management of yourself. The way you use your time affects everything that happens to you. It tells the world how much you value your life. Start by saying, "My life is precious and important, and I value every single minute and hour of it. Therefore, I resolve to use my time efficiently and well."

Time management is a series of skills, methods, and techniques. Time management is like riding a bicycle, typing on a keyboard, or playing a sport. You can learn it through repetition and practice until it becomes automatic and easy.

The Psychology of Time Management

The fact is that you feel good about yourself to the degree to which you feel that you are in control of your own life. You feel negative about yourself to the degree to which you feel you are not in control of your own life. Psychologists call this concept a "locus of control." Generally, the amount of control that you feel you have largely determines your level of happiness or unhappiness. A person with an *internal* locus of control feels that they are in charge of their own life. They feel positive, happy, optimistic, and cheerful. A person with an *external* locus of control—feeling controlled by a boss, the bills, and the circumstances outside of him- or herself—will feel negative, pessimistic, angry, and often depressed.

Time management enables you to control the direction of your life. Time management assures that your life is self-determined and under your control. Time management gives you a sense of confidence and optimism.

A Definition of Time Management

One of the best definitions of time management is "the ability to control the *sequence* of events." Managing your time requires that you determine what you do first, what you do second, and what you don't do at all. And you are always free to choose the sequence of events. In choosing the sequence of events, you choose much of what happens to you in life.

Determine Your Values

One of Murphy's Laws says that, "Before you do anything, you have to do something else first." And before you get your time under control, it is important for you to decide exactly what is most important to you in life. Good time management requires that you bring the control of the sequence of events into harmony with your values, your innermost beliefs and convictions.

Here are some questions you can ask and answer:

1. What do you value most in life?
2. Why are you doing what you are doing, rather than something else?
3. What is your reason for working where you do, at your particular job?
4. What gives you meaning and purpose in life?
5. What do you really want to do with your life?
6. If you were financially independent, and had all the time that you needed, how would you ideally spend your time?
7. What one goal, if you were absolutely guaranteed of success, would you set for your life?

Benjamin Tregoe once said that, "The very worst use of time is to do very well what need not be done at all." One of your primary goals in life is to find something that you really enjoy doing, and then to throw your whole heart into doing that job well. Even if you become excellent in doing something that you don't enjoy, you will get no satisfaction from it.

Examine your innermost values and your goals, and ask yourself what changes you could make to bring your time usage and your life priorities more into alignment with each other.

Start with Your Goals

The starting point of excellent time management is for you to become crystal clear about exactly what it is you want to accomplish. You need clear, written goals and objectives, with plans for their accomplishment. You require deadlines and subdeadlines to keep you on track, and to serve as a forcing system that keeps you on schedule.

A goal without a deadline or a timeframe is not really a goal. It is more a wish or hope. It has no energy behind it. Make detailed plans to accomplish each goal or objective. Almost all successful people are good planners. They think on paper. Whenever they have a few extra minutes, they take out a pad of paper and begin drawing up new lists and making new plans.

Time planning pays off as much as 10:1 in time savings. List every major and minor task that must be accomplished to achieve the main goal. Organize the activities in terms of time and priority. Which must be done first, and which is most important?

Review your plans regularly, and revise them when you receive new information. Be willing to make whatever changes are necessary to deal effectively with your current situation. Napoleon Hill once wrote, "The primary reason for failure is not making new plans to replace an older plan that did not work."

As Peter Drucker said, "Action without planning is the cause of every failure."

Think on Paper

Just as a pilot uses a checklist before taking off, top time managers think on paper and always work from a list. A list gives you a track to run on throughout the day. It enables you to measure your progress and helps you avoid the major time waster of *distraction*.

Make up a list of everything you have to do in the coming week. Write down what you have to do each day, preferably the evening before. Doing it ahead of time allows your subconscious mind to work on your list overnight. Often you will wake up with ideas and insights to do your job even more efficiently.

Just as a business strives to achieve the highest return on equity (ROE), your job is to achieve the highest "return on energy" (ROE). One way you accomplish high returns is by working from a list. Every minute spent in planning saves about 10 minutes in execution.

According to time management specialists, it takes about 12 minutes per day to write out a list, but these 12 minutes will save you about two hours each day (120 minutes) in actually getting the work done—a return on energy of 1,000 percent or more.

Once you have made up your list, refuse to do anything that is not on the list. If something new comes up, write it down before you do it, because act of writing down a new activity puts it in proper perspective with other things that might be more important. As you work through your list during the day, cross off each item. This simple act of crossing it off gives you a feeling of success and forward movement. It motivates you to work even more efficiently and effectively and get even more done. At the end of the day when you look at your list and see how much you've accomplished, you will feel effective and productive.

Set Priorities on Your List

Start by using the 80/20 rule on everything you do. Remember that 20 percent of what you do accounts for 80 percent of the value of everything you do, and 80 percent of your *results*. If you have a list of 10 tasks to complete in the day, two of those tasks will be worth more than the other eight put together. Always focus and concentrate on your top 20 percent.

Use the ABCDE method of time management, which is based on the fact that something is important to the degree to which it has significant potential *consequences*. Something is unimportant to the degree to which is has low or no consequences at all.

Go over your list and put one of these five letters next to each item before you begin:

- An **A** task is something that you *must* do, with high potential consequences for doing it or not doing it.
- A **B** task is something that you *should* do, when you are caught up with your A tasks, and have only mild consequences for doing it or not doing it.

- A C task is something that would be *nice to do*, but which has no consequences at all. Whether you do it makes no difference to your company or your career.
- A D activity is something that you can *delegate* to someone else. Even if you are comfortable doing it, and you've done it in the past, you must delegate everything that you can to free up your time to do just those things that have important potential consequences.
- An E item is something that should be *eliminated* altogether. It may have had some value in the past, but now it is unimportant. It may be fun and easy, but it is largely a waste of time.

Once you have organized your list with the ABCDE method, revisit the list and number each A item. Assign to it the values A-1, A-2, A-3, and so on. Do the same with your B activities. You then begin to work on your A-1 priority and discipline yourself to do nothing else until this item is completed.

You can do your B and C tasks later, but only when your A tasks have been completed. Never give in to the temptation to clear up small things first. Start on your A-1 task and then concentrate single-mindedly until it's complete.

Stay on Track

The most important question in time management is "What is the most valuable use of my time right now?" Ask yourself this question continually throughout the day, and make sure that whatever you are doing at that moment is the answer to this question.

When you first begin to ask yourself this question, you may find it a bit of an irritation. As Denis Waitley said, "Most people do things that are tension-relieving rather than activities that are goal-achieving." Because people tend to follow the path of *least resistance*, most people prefer to do what is fun, easy, and usually unimportant rather than to tackle the major tasks that can make a significant difference in their lives if they do them first, and do them well.

This principle of priorities applies to your whole life. Sometimes, the most valuable use of your time is to spend it with your family at home in the evenings, or to go to bed early and get a good night's sleep instead of watching television. What matters the most is for you to ask yourself this question regularly, and then to discipline yourself to do that task and nothing else. This habit alone will enable you to rapidly increase your productivity, performance, output, and life satisfaction.

Key Result Areas

An excellent question to ask and answer is, "Why am I on the payroll?" What exactly have you been hired to do? What are the specific, measurable results that your success and promotion depend upon?

Every job usually has about five to seven key result areas. These tasks are the ones that you absolutely, positively must accomplish if you are going to do the job you've been hired to do and get the results that are expected of you. An excellent exercise is for you to make a list of everything that you feel you have been hired to accomplish, and then take this list to your boss. Have your boss organize the list by his or her order of priority. Then, always work on what your boss considers to be the most important thing you could possibly be doing, achieving the most important results you could possibly be achieving.

As a manager, have each of your staff members come to you with a list of the reasons they feel that they are on the payroll. You should go over this list with each staff member and help them to set clear priorities on the most important work that they could be doing. From then on, manage by *priority*. The greater clarity that a person has with regard to what is the most important thing they could be doing, the happier they will be and the more they will accomplish.

Another question with regard to key results areas is, "What can I, and only I do that, if done really well, will make a real difference to my company?" Every job has certain things that only the person in that job can do. If that person doesn't do them, no one else will. But if the person in that job does them, and does them well, it can make a significant difference to both the company and to that person's career. What is it, or what are they?

Single-Minded Concentration

Concentration and single-mindedness are perhaps the most important of all time management skills. They are central to all great achievement. Your ability to concentrate single-mindedly on one thing at a time is a true measure of your desire, decision, determination, and discipline.

Focus means that you are absolutely clear about the most important task that you could be working on at the moment. Concentration means that, once you start on your most important task, you discipline yourself to continue working on that task until it is 100 percent complete. Persevere without diversion or distraction. Your ability to concentrate single-mindedly on the one task, the most important use of your time, is essential for success.

Always allow yourself enough time to complete your most important tasks. Calculate how much time it is going to take to do the job and then add 30 percent as a buffer zone. Deliberately providing a cushion of time will greatly contribute to your ability to get your most important tasks done on schedule and to a satisfactory level of quality.

Overcoming Procrastination

Procrastination is not only the thief of time, it is the thief of life. It is perhaps the greatest destroyer of human success. It is astonishing how many tasks never get completed because the individual was simply not capable of overcoming the natural human tendency to procrastinate. Fortunately, a series of time-tested techniques can help anyone in overcoming procrastination.

Bite-Sized Pieces

Make a list of all of the small tasks that you must complete in order to complete a major task. The action of breaking down a large job into a series of small jobs makes it more manageable and much easier for you to get started. You then resolve to complete one small task before you do anything else. This action often gets you launched into the job, and once you have started, you will often continue through to completion.

Salami Slice

Another variation of bite-sized pieces is for you to salami slice the task. Just as you would not attempt to eat a loaf of salami in one bite, you slice off one small bit of the job and work on that little slice until it's completed. You then go on to the next slice. This approach will often break the mental logjam of procrastination and give you the momentum to keep on working through the task.

A Sense of Urgency

One of the rarest and most valuable qualities in the world of work is a *sense of urgency*. Being known for this quality is one of the best reputations that you can have. When you become known for action-orientation, for starting and completing the job fast, you will start to attract to yourself more and more important responsibilities.

Perhaps the most powerful affirmation you can use to overcome procrastination are the words, "Do it now! Do it now! Do it now!" Whenever you feel yourself procrastinating or putting off starting or working on a major task, repeat those words to yourself until they rev you up and launch you into the job.

Creating Blocks of Time

To accomplish important tasks, you require unbroken blocks of time. The more important your work is, the more important it will be for you to set aside blocks of time to work on important projects.

Here is a rule: Do not attempt to mix the accomplishment of creative tasks with the accomplishment of functional or administrative tasks. You cannot do operational tasks and creative tasks simultaneously. They require two totally different ways of thinking and acting, which is why you sometimes hear, "You can't get any work done at work." Most of your time at work is taken up with brief meetings, conversations, phone calls, and dealing with email. You are constantly distracted by small tasks that are urgent and immediate. You never get sufficient time to focus and concentrate on major tasks.

You need 60- to 90-minute chunks of time on a regular basis to accomplish anything substantial. If it is a report or a project of some kind, you actually need about 30 minutes to get settled down and get into the task at the beginning. Only then can you really focus and concentrate, and such focus is only possible if you eliminate the distractions around you.

If you can put together *three* unbroken hours of work without interruption, you can get more done than many people accomplish in a day or two in an office where they are surrounded by interruptions and distractions.

The best chunk of time is that period you create first thing in the morning when you are fresh and most alert. You can get up at five or six in the morning and work for 60 to 90 minutes before you go to the office. Even if you get to the office late, in those 90 minutes of uninterrupted work time, you can accomplish nearly a whole day's work. Lunchtime at work is also an excellent time for you to clear up your tasks. Turn off your computer and cell phone, close your door, and work single-mindedly while everyone else has gone out for lunch.

Another way to get a chunk of time is to close your office door for certain periods each day for 60 to 90 minutes. Put a "Do not disturb" sign on the door and for one hour refuse to take any interruptions. You will be amazed at how much work you can plow through when you can concentrate single-mindedly. The greatest enemy of success today is "distraction." We are surrounded by technological "noise" that threatens to undermine our effectiveness and sabotage our careers. For this reason, one of the most important of all time management techniques is simply to "leave things off."

Check your email only twice a day. Turn off your computer so that it does not continue announcing incoming email while you are working. Turn off your telephone, or put it in silent mode and refuse to react to it every time it lights up. Have your phone calls held when you are in the office, and leave the radio off when driving so that you can use that time to think.

Controlling Interruptions

At work, interruptions are the single biggest time wasters of all. These interruptions usually occur when people walk into your office, or you walk into someone else's office, just to chat.

The biggest time waster in the world of work is other people. Continually ask, "Who wastes my time at work?" Then, if you have the courage, you should ask, "Whose time do I waste at work?" When you are a manager, you often waste other people's time by coming late to meetings, forcing everyone to wait for you, or by keeping people waiting when you have arranged to meet with them personally.

One of the best ways to minimize the time wastage of interruptions is for you to say to people who want to chat, "I'd love to talk to you right now, but I have to get *back to work*." Keep saying the words, "Back to work! Back to work! Back to work!" whenever you feel like slacking off or taking it easy. You can use these words to get yourself going, and to keep yourself going. You can use these words to break off a conversation by telling the other person that you have to get back to work. No one will ever try to hold you back from your work.

Batching Your Tasks

Batching your tasks simply means doing several similar jobs at the same time. Because everything you do involves a learning curve, when you do a series of identical or similar tasks all in a row, the learning curve reduces the time to do each subsequent task by as much as 80 percent. Batch writing letters, emails, and other correspondence together and do them all at once. Batch your phone calls and return them all at once. If you have to interview a number of people, do them consecutively.

By doing similar tasks all at once, you can dramatically reduce the amount of time that it takes to get through all of those similar tasks.

You can add one or two hours of output and increased productivity to your day in this way.

Organize Your Work Space

Organize your work space and clear your desk before you begin. Don't let paperwork pile up around you. Put all your documents away into the appropriate files and deal only with your current work. Try to have only one item in front of you whenever possible.

Think of your office as that of a dentist, doctor, or lawyer. The top professionals in every field keep a tidy and highly ordered work space at all times. They clean up and reorder their workspace as they go through their day.

Get organized and stay organized. Make sure your office supplies and materials are fully stocked. Once you start work, be sure that you have everything at hand to complete the task.

Delegate everything you possibly can to others who can do the tasks as well or better than you. Become excellent at delegation, outsourcing, and eliminating. These activities expand your capacity and output from what you can do to what you can manage. Learn the skills of correct delegation, beginning with choosing the right person to handle each task. Provide timelines, deadlines, standards of performance, and a regular schedule.

Maintain Balance in Your Life

The most important factors for happiness, health, and high productivity in life are balance and moderation. As Shakespeare said, "There is more to life than simply increasing its speed." The main purpose of learning and practicing time management is to enhance and improve the overall quality of your life. It is to increase the amount of pleasure and happiness that you experience. Improving your overall quality of life should be your main goal.

Your health is extremely important. No success in business will compensate for ill health. Take time to eat the right foods and get regular exercise and the proper rest and recreation. Sometimes the best use of your time is to go to bed early and get a good night's sleep.

Finally, and most important of all, you must take time for your relationships. The people you care about and who care about you are the most important parts of your life. Never allow yourself to get so caught up in your work that you ignore the importance of those key relationships—your spouse, children, and close friends.

An excellent life is one that is in balance. If you spend ample time preserving and enhancing the quality of your relationships, you will find that you get more joy, satisfaction, success, and fulfillment out of your life than if you allowed your work to pull your life out of balance. A wise old doctor once observed, "I never spoke to a businessman on his death bed who said that he wished he had spent more time at the office."

Action Exercises

1. Determine your three most important business goals, those goals or results that make more of a difference to your success than any other.
2. Determine the three most important tasks you do to achieve your most important goals.
3. Determine your three most important values or organizing principles in life. What is most important to you?
4. Make a list each day of everything you have to do, and then organize it by priority using the 80/20 rule and the ABCDE method.
5. Create chunks of time each week when you can work without interruption on your most important projects.
6. Delegate everything possible to free up time to do those things that only you can do. What are they?
7. Keep your life in balance. Organize your time so that you spend ample time with your family and on personal activities.

CHAPTER TWELVE

THE DISCIPLINE OF PERSONAL EXCELLENCE

"The starting point of all achievement is desire. Weak desires bring weak results, just as a small fire makes a small amount of heat."

—Napoleon Hill

Two hundred years ago, when the industrial revolution began, most of the world was poor. Over the past 200 years, we've gone through a technological revolution with the advent of the steam engine and electricity right up to our current amazing technologies. High technology has vastly reduced poverty in most of the Western world and has created more wealth for more people than has ever been dreamed possible in all of human history.

But the fact is that it's not technology alone that has brought about these changes. It has not been just a technological revolution but a *managerial* revolution. It is the managers of enterprises and organizations at all levels who have been responsible for the great bursts in progress. Technology has always followed managerial development.

When Vince Lombardi took over the Green Bay Packers, he was asked, "How are you going to change the way this team operates? Are you going to bring in new plays and ideas on how to run the ball?" He said "No, we're just going to become brilliant on the basics." For you to succeed greatly as a manager and leader, you must also become brilliant on the basics. Often, a single key skill that you develop can dramatically improve your effectiveness and your ability to get results.

Become an Excellent Manager

What is an excellent manager? An excellent manager is somebody who achieves superior results by consistently getting the best out of him- or herself and by releasing the potential of others so they can make their maximum contribution to the organization.

The strength of any organization is determined by the quality of its managers at all levels. They are the "officer corps" of the corporate army. What they do and how well they do it is the key determinant of corporate success. The most conservative studies estimate that the average person works at less than 50 percent of capacity, and sometimes less than 40 percent or 30 percent! A good manager creates an environment in which the average person functions at 60, 70, 80, or 90 percent, and occasionally close to 100 percent of capacity, and makes a massive rather than average contribution to the organization.

Ask the Right Questions

The starting point of managerial effectiveness is asking and answering the right questions, over and over. Excellent managers are highly aware of the answers to the important questions: *Why are you on the payroll? What have you been hired to accomplish?* A good manager is continually asking and answering these questions, for himself, and for each staff member.

Good managers are extremely *result-oriented*, versus process- or activity-oriented. They always have their eye on the ball, on the results they've been hired to produce.

Another question you can ask and answer is, *"What is the unique contribution that only you can make?"* What can you and only you contribute to your organization that if done well will make a significant difference? Most people spend 80 percent of their time on the 80 percent of their work that only contributes 20 percent of their value. Top-performing managers always concentrate on the few things that, if done really well, will make a real difference.

Questions you can ask, especially if you are not making the progress you want, or you are experiencing resistance, include "What are we trying to do? How are we trying to do it? Could there be a better way?" Continually asking these questions widens your perspective, expands your range of understanding, and brings you answers, ideas, and insights that help you to be more effective and to make a more valuable contribution in a shorter period of time.

Focus on Key Result Areas

Your key result areas are your most significant areas of contribution. They are the field of performance of the manager. The focus on key result areas is the key to your effectiveness, your future, and your career. Each of the seven key results areas for managers is important. In each position of management, one of these key result areas is usually more important than any other at the moment.

Customer Service

The first key result area is *customer needs*. As a manager, you have three customers that you have to satisfy to be successful. The first customer you have to serve is your boss. As long as you please your boss and give the boss what he or she wants in the form that he or she wants, your job will be secure.

The second customer that you have to satisfy is the external customer, the customer who has to use what your company or department produces. It could be an outside customer or it could be another department within the organization.

Your third customer is your staff. Good managers serve their people to help them be better in accomplishing their jobs. This idea is the reason for the popularity of what is called "servant leadership."

Profit and Loss

The second key result area is *economics*. All organizations are constrained by economics of some kind. By that we mean that you're continually working to either increase revenues or to decrease costs. You are continually thinking in terms of the cost of inputs relative to the cost of outputs. You are continually striving to increase profits, to increase the return on investment of time and money.

Strive for Excellence

The third key result area in business is *quality*. The quality of your work is absolutely essential to your success, as is the quality of the products and services your company produces. Quality improvement should be going on every day. The formula for business success is CANEI, which stands for "continuous and never-ending improvement." You must emphasize quality, discuss quality, and continually ask how you can improve the quality of what you do for your customers.

Achieve More with Less

The fourth key result area is *productivity*. How can you increase your personal productivity, the productivity of your staff, and the productivity of your business while decreasing or constraining costs?

Faster, Better, Cheaper

The fifth key result area in business is *innovation*, continually seeking new ideas for products and services or ways to do the work faster, better, or cheaper. Innovation includes new ways of doing things, new approaches, new products, new services, and new methods and processes. You must be thinking about innovation and the future, and get your people thinking about it, all the time.

Grow Your People

The sixth key result area is *people growth*. How do you grow your people? According to recent research, the payoff in people training is as much as 20:1 or even 30:1. You get a $20 or $30 return for every dollar you invest in training. The top 20 percent of companies in terms of profitability in each industry spend 3 percent or more of their gross revenues training their people.

People growth is an essential part of growing your company. Almost 85 cents of each dollar of operational costs is spent on salaries and benefits. On average, companies spend less than one cent of each of those dollars in training the people who generate those revenues.

Grow the Business

The seventh key result area in business is *organizational development*. Organizational development means doing the things that create a positive and harmonious organizational climate. These factors are the ones that make people feel happy to work there and produce at their best.

You should be continually asking yourself what you can do to improve performance in each of these areas. Which of these areas constitutes the 20 percent of issues that account for 80 percent of your problems? What are the 20 percent of opportunities that offer the greatest potential for the future? Excellent managers focus their efforts on the most important key result areas that affect their business at the current time. What are yours right now?

Set Standards of Performance

You need standards of performance (SOPs) for each job and for each function in your area of responsibility. People can usually hit a target if they can see it, but nobody can hit a target they can't see. These standards need to be specific, measurable, and time-bounded. When you ask someone to do something, you have to tell them exactly *what* it is that you want, *how* you're going to measure it, and *when* you want it done by. One of the most important rules of management is "What gets measured gets done."

Standards of performance must be the basis for rewards and promotion. Rewards in an excellent organization go to performance, to excellence, to sales, and to achievement. Rewards must be based on performance alone. Once you have established standards of performance, you must *inspect what you expect*. Inspect, monitor, control, and assure compliance with your performance standards.

You must recognize the difference between delegation and abdication. Even if you delegate the job, you are still responsible for its successful completion. It is therefore essential that you inspect what you expect. When you inspect what you expect, people see that you consider it important that they maintain those standards.

Managing by Objectives

Management by objectives is a vital tool you can use to increase your output and build the competence of your subordinates. Most managers don't use MBO, or don't use it correctly when they use it. MBO is effective with *competent* people who have already demonstrated an ability to do the job well. When you have a new task, you sit down with them to discuss and agree on the job that has to be done.

You agree on measurements and standards of performance as well as the schedule for completion. When you use MBO to assign an objective or goal you say, "This is what needs to be done. This is how we will measure it, and here is the timeline." You make it clear that this person is responsible for the job, but if he or she needs any help or assistance, you are available to that person at any time.

You then leave the person alone to do the job. Allow the staff member to accomplish the goal using his or her own ideas, methods, and techniques. Even if you think that you would do it differently, you must give the person the freedom to decide how to get it done. And finally, arrange to review progress on a regular basis. Set a schedule for reporting. Get together once a week or once a month to catch up.

The management by objectives system is a powerful way for you to pass off critical areas of responsibility or key result areas to staff. It is also a powerful way to grow people in confidence and competence.

Managing by Exception

Management by exception is an excellent time saver and people builder. Once you have given an assignment and you've made it clear, measurable, and time-bounded, you then tell the person, "You only need to come back to me if a variance from what we've agreed upon occurs."

If everything is going well and the job is on schedule, he or she doesn't have to report to you. But if a problem or challenge does arise, that person can come back to you for comment or advice. In management by exception, "no news is good news." This method of managing, to be used only with competent people, is a great time saver for you, and a people builder for your employee.

Delegate Effectively

Your ability to delegate will be a critical determinant of your success in management. Delegation allows you to increase your span of control from what you can do personally, to what you can control. Good delegators get more and more done, and are therefore assigned more and more people to whom they can delegate.

The first step in delegating is for you to match the task to the skills of the employee. One of the big mistakes in delegation is assigning a task to someone who does not have the skills, confidence, ability, or the motivation to accomplish it.

When you delegate, explain the results that you want and *why* you want those results. The why is often more important than the how. A person who knows why you want a certain job to be done will be much more capable of making decisions and more creative and innovative in accomplishing the result you desire.

When delegating, you also need to explain your preferred method of working. This approach is different from management by objectives. In delegating, you tell the person how you think it should be done based on your own experience. This method is just your preferred method and not engraved in stone. But it gives them a process to follow. Then make him or her 100 percent responsible for the task. Increased responsibility is a powerful way to build competence and confidence in people. Resist the temptation to look over the person's shoulder. Resist the temptation to interfere. Once you have assigned the task, don't take it back.

Finally, schedule regular meetings for review. In this way, you keep on top of things. You get feedback on how appropriate the task is for this person. Sometimes you might delegate a task that is beyond the person's capability. You can then revise or reduce the scope of the job.

At other times, the task will be too much, and the person to whom the task was delegated will feel in over his or her head. You will need to reorganize the task, give the person additional input or resources, shift the load, or take back part of the task.

Achieving Managerial Leverage

One of your goals as a manager is to increase the quality and quantity of your output relative to your input. You can use any of several ways to increase or even *multiply* your productivity as a manager.

- Do things you are better at. Delegate things that you're not good at. Do more of the things you do easily and well, those tasks in your areas of strength. Because you can do these tasks faster and more efficiently, you can make a bigger contribution.
- Teach, train, and delegate to others. The more you teach, train, and delegate, you more you can get done of your own work.
- Do more important things. Set priorities and concentrate on the most valuable use of your time.
- Simplify your work. One of the best ways to minimize the amount of work you have to do is to get rid of certain jobs or parts of jobs that are no longer essential. Eliminate unnecessary steps and consolidate jobs. Avoid activities that do not contribute to your key result areas. Always be seeking ways to get more important things done in less time.

Build Team Spirit

Team building is an essential skill of effective managers and a key ability required for promotion. The ability to build and work with an effective team is also one of the key qualities that companies look for when seeking out prospective CEOs. It is absolutely essential to your success.

Here are three ideas for building a top team:

1. First, mutually establish an overarching goal or mission for the team—something challenging and exciting. Make it an inspiring concept that makes people want to make a real contribution to the results desired.
2. Second, hold weekly meetings in which each person tells what he or she is doing. This simple activity creates better communication and interaction between the team members. Be sure that everyone gets a chance to tell everyone else what they are working on and how it is going. And especially, explain to everyone how his or her job fits into the "big picture" and how it affects others.
3. Third, celebrate successes. One of the key functions of the manager is to orchestrate celebrations for special occasions, birthdays, and achievements. When people are praised and celebrated they feel more committed and dedicated to the company, and so do the other team members.

Make Better Decisions

Decisiveness is a key quality of effective managers. No promotion or advancement is possible until a person develops the ability to make good decisions quickly. As a manager, you will spend 50 percent to 60 percent of your time solving problems and making decisions. Your ability in this area will, as much as any other factor, determine the success of your career as a manager. Fortunately, problem solving and decision making are skills that you can learn.

Begin by defining clearly what you're trying to avoid, preserve, or accomplish. What are you trying to accomplish? What is your goal? When you are faced with a problem, get the facts before deciding. What exactly has happened? How did it happen? Why did it happen? What are all the possible solutions to this problem, or possible courses of action?

Once you have the information, decide quickly. Eighty percent of all decisions should be made when the question comes up. Only 20 percent of decisions require more information. If you cannot make an immediate decision, set a deadline. Resolve to make a decision on the subject by a certain time. Make a decision, assign responsibility for carrying out the decision, take action on the decision, and then follow up and make sure the action is carried out. Often, any decision is better than no decision at all. If you receive new information on the problem or decision, be prepared to change your decision or do something else.

Most of all, focus on the solution rather than the problem. The more you think about solutions, about what can be done, about what actions you can take, the more solutions you will come up with, and the more creative you will become.

Remove Obstacles to Performance

Every work process encounters obstacles that limit the amount of work that can be done. The removal of these "limiting steps" is often the fastest way to increase output. One of the primary jobs of the manager is to identify obstacles to job completion and find ways to remove them.

Begin by developing absolute clarity about your most important goal. Then ask, "Why haven't we achieved this goal already? What is holding us back? Of all the factors that are holding us back, what is the biggest obstacle, and how could we remove it?" The answer is called your "key constraint" or "limiting factor." Once you have identified what it is, you then focus single-mindedly on alleviating this constraint or limit. You focus day and night until you have solved the problem or removed the obstacle that is holding you back from achieving greater success. Get rid of it and get it out of the way.

Employ the 80/20 rule. One or two problems or obstructions cause most of your problems in achieving results. What are your main obstacles to accomplishment? Sometimes by removing the number one obstacle in your path, whatever is standing between you and your most important business goal, you can make more progress in a week or a month than you could make in a year doing other things or solving smaller problems. As Goethe said, "The main thing is to make the main thing the main thing."

The obstacles between you and outstanding business success usually have to do with product or service quality, or they have to do with people skills and abilities. Sometimes the major obstacle to the growth of your company is the lack of a key person or the presence of an incompetent person who should not be in your company any more.

Communicate with Clarity

Eighty-five percent of managerial success is determined by the manager's ability to communicate effectively with others. Fortunately, the ability to communicate well one-on-one, in meetings, and in front of a group is a learnable skill. You can take specific actions to be a better communicator.

First of all learn how to *write well*. Written communication requires clarity, brevity, simplicity, and accuracy. Your writing skills can be improved through learning and practice. Numerous excellent courses and books on business communications are available to help you in this area.

Second, learn how to *speak on your feet*. Learn how to stand up in front of an audience and speak effectively and persuasively. You can join Toastmasters International, go to Dale Carnegie, or take a course in professional speaking. People who can speak on their feet advance more rapidly in their careers as managers than people who cannot. Learn how to speak well and give good presentations at meetings within the company and outside the company.

Third, learn how to *sell your ideas*. All top managers are good at selling ideas. When you are selling your ideas to others, begin by asking what is in it for them. Always present your ideas in terms of benefits for the listeners, in terms of improvement of some kind, and doing things better.

Whenever you introduce a new idea to others, expect resistance at the beginning. Instead of rushing to your recommendation or conclusion, you say, "I've been thinking about ways that we can improve how we do things in this area. I've come up with an idea that might enable us to save money or cut costs. What do you think of this idea?" Then give them time to think it over.

The average person needs 72 hours to incorporate a new idea into his or her way of thinking. If you present a new idea and demand an immediate decision, almost invariably the answer will be *no*. But when you allow people to think about it for two or three days, they will gradually begin to see the possibilities in it.

Achieve Personal Excellence

Commit to excellence and personal pride. Nothing is more likely to affect your career more than your committing to becoming personally excellent at what you do.

Every organization has two routes to the top. One route is through *performance*. The other route is through *politics*. And every study we've seen in the past few years says that, if you try to get to the top through politics, you will almost invariably be derailed somewhere along the way. But if you work to get to the top through excellent performance, almost everyone in the organization will help you. These people include those above you, others at your level, and people below you. Your high road to success is always for you to commit to becoming the best manager you can possibly be.

Set standards of excellence for yourself and for everyone under you. Encourage, recognize, and reward quality work. Remember that you will always be judged on the basis of the quality of the work of people who have been entrusted to you to manage or supervise.

Celebrate success and achievement. Give rewards and prizes. Catch people doing something right. Praise people whenever they do something well or when they go the extra mile in their work.

Most importantly, lead by example. Look upon yourself as the standard bearer of your department or unit or company. Always walk, talk, and deal with people as you would like them to act toward each other. If you look upon yourself as a role model, you will put yourself on the high road to leadership in your organization and in your life.

Leadership Is Learnable

Successful managers are made, not born. You can become an excellent manager and leader in your work and your life if you learn and practice the behaviors, methods, and techniques of other successful managers and leaders.

The ideas contained in this book are based on more than 30 years of research and experience in large and small companies. If you recognize that you are deficient in any of these areas, resolve right now, today, to do something about it. Read a book, take a seminar, listen to an audio program, or ask for advice from someone you respect. Your career success may depend on it.

Action Exercises

1. Decide today to become an excellent executive. What one skill would help you the most to get better results in your position?
2. Decide today to become an excellent public speaker and communicator. What would be your first step?
3. Manage your time more efficiently. What could you start doing more of, or less of, to be more productive?
4. What tasks should you delegate to free up more of your time, and to whom should you delegate these tasks?
5. What is the most important decision you have to make right now, and what are you going to do?

6. What is the most important key result area of your position or your business you should concentrate on improving?

7. Practice management by objectives with your competent staff. What large task or area of activity should you turn over completely to someone else?

INDEX

ABOUT THE AUTHORS

Brian Tracy is one of the top business speakers, management trainers, and inspirational "gurus" in the world today. He has delivered more than 5,000 presentations to 5 million people in 60 countries.

Each year, Brian addresses more than 250,000 people in large and small businesses, and audiences ranging from 100 to 10,000. He is the author of 60 books that have been translated into 42 languages and are sold in 56 countries.

As president of Business Growth Strategies, Brian oversees the on-line video-based training program that teaches management, sales, business success, and time management skills. He has produced more than 500 audio and video learning programs and is the president of three companies based in San Diego, California.

Brian is the developer and presenter of the "Two-Day MBA," a powerful, practical program built around 10 key business principles that are essential for increased sales and profitability.

More than 1,000 large companies worldwide have benefited from Brian's teaching and training in the subjects of leadership, strategy, management effectiveness, motivation, hiring and firing, and personal excellence. His 14-book series on management excellence is sold worldwide.

Dr. Peter Chee is the president and CEO of ITD World, a leading multinational corporation for human resource development. Dr. Chee has trained and developed leaders from more than 80 countries, and with his leadership contribution over 26 years, ITD World has established itself as a global learning solutions expert.

The coinventor of The Coaching Principles (TCP) the Situational Coaching Model (SCM) and Achievers Coaching Techniques (ACT), Dr. Chee is a chief mentor coach and master trainer for Jack Canfield, Dr. John Maxwell, Brian Tracy, and Zig Ziglar programs. Dr. Chee holds a doctor of business administration degree from the University of South Australia (UniSA), an MSc in Training and HRM from the University of Leicester, UK, and was also a graduate of the Chartered Institute of Marketing, UK.

Best-selling and award winning authors who have worked in close partnership with Dr. Chee include Brian Tracy, Dr. William Rothwell, who has authored more than 80 books, and Dr. Jack Canfield, the world's leading success coach who holds a place in the *Guinness World Records* for the most books on the *New York Times* Bestseller List with of 210 books and 125 million copies in print. Dr. Chee and Jack Canfield are coauthors of *Coaching for Breakthrough Success.* He is the coauthor of *12 Disciplines of Leadership Excellence* with Brian Tracy and the co-author of *Becoming an Effective Mentoring Leader* with Dr. William Rothwell.

Dr. Chee is a Baden Powell Fellow of the World Scout Foundation, an honor bestowed by the king of Sweden. He was the president of ARTDO International, a nonprofit professional umbrella body that brings together renowned national HRD bodies, governments, and multinational companies active in HRD work globally. With his commitment to a societal-oriented philosophy, the ITD World's "love thy nation" campaigns have channeled sizable funds to support the needy sections of many national societies. Dr. Chee has fulfilled many of his dreams. His purpose is to transform leaders and change the world with love for God and people. He lives close to the sea and hills of the beautiful island of Penang with his wife Eunice and daughter Adelina.

BRIAN TRACY
Speaker, Trainer and Seminar Leader

Brian is one of the top professional speakers in the world, addressing more than 250,000 people each year. Brian has given more than 5,000 talks and seminars and has worked with more than 1,000 companies worldwide.

His talks are fast-moving, informative, enjoyable and entertaining. Brian has a wonderful ability to customize each talk for his particular audience. He presents a series of great ideas and strategies with a rare combination of fact, humor, insights and practical concepts that audience members can apply immediately to get better results.

Brian's talks can be customized to your company's situation, goals and vision. Here's just one of the topics Brian can cover in your event:

High-Performance Leadership

Brian gives managers a series of proven strategies they can use immediately to get better results in every area of their businesses. They learn how to think strategically, manage time more efficiently, select the right people, communicate effectively and build peak performing teams; highly informative, loaded with content and both funny and motivational. Brian has given this program in hundreds of companies worldwide.

Other Topics Include:

- High Performance Selling
- Performing At Your Best!
- Doubling Your Productivity, Achieving Your Goals

12 Disciplines of Leadership
FREE RESOURCES

Brian Tracy has created these valuable resources
to help you lead you and your company to excellence.

FREE RESOURCE #1:

7 Responsibilities of Leaders
PDF Report

There are 7 key responsibilities of leadership in
any organization, and your ability in each of
these areas determines your value to yourself
and your contribution to your organization.
This detailed report will help you identify
and achieve your sales, growth, and profitability goals – easier than ever before!

FREE RESOURCE #2:
Leadership Questionnaire

Discover how to address all major strategic and
management issues that most, present-day
leaders face. This Leadership Questionnaire
will help you define what elements are important to the success of your company and
how to get your staff on the same page.

FREE RESOURCE #3:

21 Great Ways to Become an Outstanding Manager

No one ever said management was easy. The ability to lead and manage a team in order to get top results is a true skill, and the top managers seem to do just that.

Brian Tracy's audio program, *21 Great Ways to Become an Outstanding Manager,* will teach you how to manage, motivate and build a high performance team. Turn yourself into one of the most valuable assets of your company and open the doors to your success as an elite manager!

FREE RESOURCE #4:

Leadership Video Training Series

Take your management career to the next level and save yourself years of hard work on your journey to the top. In this Leadership Video Training Series, you'll learn all the secrets to sharpen your management skills and lead your company to success.

You will receive 5 valuable videos on the following topics:

- Become an Excellent Manager
- Train and Develop Your People
- Create a Caring Work Environment
- Staff Well at All Levels
- Create Great Morale in Your Organization

Master the Skills and Techniques Used by the Top-Ranked Managers in the World....

FREE WEBINAR & eBOOK:
How to Write a Book and Become a Published Author

Have you ever wanted to write a book and inspire readers to improve their own lives by sharing your experiences and your message?

If you just KNOW that you have a story inside of you, but aren't sure how to turn that story into a book, then this FREE WEBINAR is for YOU.

In This Free Webinar, You'll Learn:

■ My PROVEN 4-step process for writing a book and getting it published. I use this EVERY time I write a book — and you can use it too.

■ How to decide what you should write about — and it may not be what you think

■ The part of the process that's even more difficult than the writing

■ 4 keys to marketing your book idea — miss any one of these and you may never get a publisher

How Do I Register?

DR. PETER CHEE
Mentor Coach, Speaker and Trainer

HIGHLIGHTS

- Trained and developed leaders from over 80 countries with over 26 years international experience.
- Author of *Coaching for Breakthrough Success* with Jack Canfield.
- Inventor of the Situational Coaching Model (SCM) The Coaching Principles (TCP) and Achievers Coaching Techniques (ACT).
- Author of *Becoming an Effective Mentoring Leader* with William J. Rothwell who is an award winning author of over 80 books and Professor at Pennsylvania State University.

- Author of *The 12 Disciplines of Leadership Excellence* with Brian Tracy who has written 56 books in 38 languages.
- Doctor of Business Administration Degree from the University of South Australia, MSc. in Training and HRM from the University of Leicester, UK.
- Chief Mentor Coach and developer of the Certified Coaching and Mentoring Professional (CCMP) program.
- President and CEO of ITD World: The Global Learning Solutions Expert.

AREAS OF EXPERTISE

Personal Excellence & The Success Principles-Techniques for Breakthrough Results
Coaching & Mentoring Excellence
Leadership & Team Excellence
Motivation & Performance Management
Work, Life and Time Management

COACHES, MENTORS & SPEAKERS BUREAU
ENRICHING YOU WITH OUTSTANDING RESULTS

AT ITD WORLD WE ENSURE THAT YOUR NEEDS AND OBJECTIVES ARE MATCHED WITH THE BEST RESOURCE PERSON

We have over 238 programs and more than 100 dedicated mega gurus, top international resource persons, trainers, speakers, coaches, mentors and consultants from around the world and many of them are featured on this site:

www.itdworld.com/speakers
www.itdworld.com/coachesmentors

CERTIFIED COACHING & MENTORING PROFESSIONAL (CCMP) PROGRAM

with

Certificate in Performance Coaching
Certificate in Advanced Coaching and Mentoring

"The Certificate in Performance Coaching is one of the only truly international courses in Asia that is recognized and approved by ICF (International Coaching Federation) the world's leading professional non-profit body for coaching. Mentoring, coaching and growing people is one of the most fulfilling and rewarding work of a lifetime"

- William J. Rothwell Ph.D

PROGRAM MAP

THE 3 PHASES

Phase 1
Course 1 & 2: 4 days + Assignments

Phase 2
Course 3 & 4: 5 days + Assignments

Phase 3
Coaching & Mentoring Action Project: 120 days + Conformance to Professional Ethics and Continuous Professional Development (CPD)

THE 3 AWARDS

CERTIFICATE IN PERFORMANCE COACHING

CERTIFICATE IN ADVANCED COACHING AND MENTORING

CERTIFIED COACHING & MENTORING PROFESSIONAL (CCMP)

WHAT MAKES THE CCMP PROGRAM OUTSTANDING?

- Brings together program intellect and design from the world's top authorities in coaching, mentoring and peak performance: Dr. William Rothwell, Dr. Jack Canfield, Dr. Peter Chee and Thomas G Crane.
- Recognized and approved by ICF (International Coaching Federation), the world's leading professional non-profit professional body for coaching.
- Uses training, coaching, mentoring, action and experiential learning all in one comprehensive results-based learning solution.
- Includes cutting-edge tools, learning materials and best-selling books to support effective learning, application and for ongoing research.

- A continuous learning intervention over 5 months that leads to professional mastery of coaching and mentoring. Delivered by the most experienced and competent facilitators and trainers.
- Learning support provided by a mentor coach throughout the action learning project phase.
- Comprehensive and effective assessment of each participant to demonstrate attainment of bottom-line results from coaching and mentoring.
- The 3 awards obtained throughout the program offers great reward for achievement and motivation to learn, apply and succeed.

For full details pls go to http://www.itdworld.com/itdphp/competency/itd_competency_CCMP.php

The Global Learning Solutions Expert

www.itdworld.com

Approved Coach Specific Training Hours
International Coach Federation

International Coach Federation